78.50

22329

71

B

KEY TEXTS

Classic Studies in the History of Ideas

THE PHILOSOPHY OF NIETZSCHE

Abraham Wolf

THOEMMES
PRESS

© Thoemmes Press 1994

Published in 1994 by
Thoemmes Press
11 Great George Street
Bristol BS1 5RR
England

ISBN 1 85506 353 0

This is a reprint of the 1915 Edition

Publisher's Note

CONTENTS

PREFACE

THE following pages contain the substance of a
course of three lectures delivered at the University
of London, University College, last February. The
object of the lectures was to present the salient
ideas of Nietzsche in an impartial and coherent
manner, and with a minimum of technical terms.
The general appreciation expressed by the large
audiences who attended the lectures has encouraged
me to believe that the lectures have not entirely
failed to achieve their modest purpose.

The references to Nietzsche's writings, given in
the foot-notes, should be easily verifiable in any
edition of his works. But for the special convenience of English readers I have also given in
brackets the pages of the English translation of
Nietzsche's Works, edited by Dr. Oscar Levy.
The quotations are mostly taken from this serviceable translation.

A. WOLF.

Chesham Bois,
May, 1915.

" In future let no one concern himself about me, but only about the things for which I lived."—NIETZSCHE.

THE PHILOSOPHY OF NIETZSCHE

CHAPTER I

NIETZSCHE AND THE WAR

SINCE the outbreak of the war Nietzsche has acquired unenviable notoriety. His name has become a byword among us. Thanks to the influence of the Press and the pulpit he is commonly regarded as one of the villains in the terrible drama that is now claiming nearly all the world for its stage. True, Nietzsche's activities ceased in 1888, and he died in 1900. But his spirit, it is said, is still playing its villainous part, and keen-sighted seers can see it haunting the bloody battle-fields in the East and in the West. For " the evil that men do lives after them."

This picture, however, is a work of creative imagination, unrestrained by knowledge. It is a vision only granted to those who have the gift of seeing what is not there. To those who really know Nietzsche few things can appear more unwarranted and absurd than the constant coupling of his name with those of Bernhardi and Treitschke as one of the principal inspirers of the present war,

B   9

which an enterprising bookseller in the Strand has actually christened the " Euro-Nietzschean " war. Whatever criticisms may be made against Nietzsche and his views—and indeed a good many criticisms may well be made—the charge that he wittingly incited Germany to a war of aggression is unfounded. So far from encouraging German megalomania, he was one of its most scathing critics. To his credit be it said that he long ago discerned the evil tendencies which have led up to this tragic climax, and he gravely warned Europe, and Germany above all, against the bitter harvest that might be reaped some day from those evil seeds. German pride of race he denounced as a " mendacious race-swindle."[1] German pride of intellect he met with the humiliating taunt that, in spite of their bookishness, the German people are boorish and devoid of genuine culture. In the very hour of their greatest triumph, in 1871, he dared tell his conquering countrymen that the culture of vanquished France was incomparably superior to theirs. Again and again he denounced German state-idolatry, its militarism, its fanatical patriotism, its high politics, the Bismarckian worship of success, and the arrogant creed of *Deutsch-*

[1] *Peoples and Countries*, §§ 20 f. (vol. xiii, p. 226).

land, Deutschland über alles.[1] He remonstrated with his compatriots for putting a policy of " national and political lunacy "[2] in the place of the culture which they formerly possessed, and which first made other European nations interested in them. And long before the " mailed fist " and " shining armour " made their public appearance Nietzsche rebuked the tactlessness of German statesmen. " German public utterances," he complained, " are not inspired by German music, but by the new tone of tasteless arrogance. Almost in every speech of the foremost German statesman, even when he makes himself heard through his imperial mouthpiece, there is an accent which the ear of a foreigner repudiates with aversion."[3] Nor did Nietzsche overlook the mischief that was spread by certain German historians. In caustic terms he denounced the "political puppets" and " tyrannical politicians " who " altered and touched up " history, embellishing it with alluring fictions which " entice the brave to rashness and the enthusiastic to fanaticism," so that there is constant danger of murder and war.[4] And turn-

[1] *Human All-Too-Human*, i, § 68 (p. 80), and next reference to *Ecce Homo*.   [2] *The Dawn of Day*, § 190 (p. 187 f.).
[3] *Joyful Wisdom*, § 104 (p. 143 f.).
[4] *Thoughts out of Season*, vol. ii—" The Use and Abuse of History," § ii (p. 20 f.).

ing to Treitschke more particularly he exclaims contemptuously : " There is such a thing as writing history according to the lights of Imperial Germany ; there is also anti-Semitic history ; there is also history written with an eye to the Court, and Herr von Treitschke is not ashamed of himself.'" The new ambition of German *Weltpolitik* appeared to Nietzsche to be associated with a good deal of charlatanism. He strongly protested against it, and expostulated with his countrymen vehemently for sacrificing the German spirit to the German Empire. He cannot, therefore, be justly accused of having inspired, or encouraged, or even quietly approved of German jingoism.

As a matter of fact, Nietzsche's social and political theories were altogether opposed to the kind of fanatical patriotism which finds vent in international animosities—*Vaterländerei* he called it contemptuously.' He was essentially a broad-minded citizen of the world, " a good European " (as he styled himself), anxious to see the different nations working in friendly rivalry towards the advancement of mankind, and the development of the highest types of men.

---

[1] *Ecce Homo*—Passage relating to " The Case of Wagner," § 2 (p. 123 f).
[2] *Joyful Wisdom*, § 347 (p. 286).

He was by no means entirely averse to warfare.
He even looked upon it as a hope and remedy " for
nations that are growing weak and contemptible "
—though only as a last hope and brutal remedy.
But he did not hold that *live* people should go in
for such drastic treatment.[1] On the contrary, he
pointed out that war generally involves the sacrifice
of the best and bravest, who naturally expose
themselves to the greatest dangers. Nor is this the
only evil consequence of war to which he drew
attention. War, he observed, betrays people into
exaggerated self-esteem : each side claims for itself
a monopoly of good taste, sound judgment, and all
the virtues.[2] Nor, he thinks, is the result ever
satisfactory ; the victors are apt to become stupid,
and the vanquished revengeful.[3] Mankind, he insists, have " quite other and higher tasks " which
make " the rough Roman patriotism either something dishonourable or a sign of being behind the
times."[4] He even objects to an excessive pre-
occupation with military matters in times of peace.
Conscription may be a good thing as an antidote
against decadence ; but there are, he thinks, other

---

[1] *Human All-Too-Human*, vol. ii—" The Wanderer and His
Shadow," § 187 (p. 288).
[2] *The Will to Power*, vol. i, § 348 (p. 281).
[3] *Human All-Too-Human*, vol. i, § 444 (p. 322).
[4] *Human All-Too-Human*, vol. i, § 442 (p. 321).

preventives of decadence which do not entail such a waste of energy as is incurred when " year after year the ablest, strongest, and most industrious men are withdrawn, in extraordinary numbers, from their proper occupations and callings, to be turned into soldiers.'"[1]

Moreover, he had his suspicions about the honesty and the wisdom of the doctrine of "Armed Peace." His criticism of the view is well worth noting. " No government," says Nietzsche, " will nowadays admit that it maintains an army in order to satisfy occasionally its passion for conquest. The army, it is said, is intended only for purposes of defence. But this means that each state in turn claims to be more moral than its neighbours, whose assumed eagerness for unjust attack makes defensive preparations necessary. The neighbouring states, however, also disavow aggressive intentions, and ostensibly maintain their armies likewise, not for offensive, but only for defensive purposes. Hence virtually each state accuses its neighbouring states of criminal hypocrisy and cunning, of lying in wait for it in order to pounce upon it unexpectedly." Nietzsche condemns the whole attitude as inhuman : it is a constant challenge and provoca-

[1] *Human All-Too-Human*, vol. i, § 481 (p. 353).

tion to war; it is as bad as war, or even worse. The so-called armed peace, he maintains, is the expression of a bellicose disposition which trusts neither itself nor its neighbour, and refuses to lay down arms partly from hatred and partly from fear. " But," protests Nietzsche, " better to perish than to hate and fear; and thrice better to perish than to make oneself hated and feared!" He maintains that the whole policy of armed peace must be abjured as completely as the lust of conquest. And he finds fault with the liberal representatives of the people for working only for " a gradual reduction of armaments." Such efforts, such half measures, are vain : " the tree of military glory can only be destroyed at one swoop, with one stroke of lightning." And since lightning comes only from above, he can but hope that some day a nation renowned in war and victories, and distinguished by the highest military skill and organization, will deliberately proclaim : " Let us break our swords," and will demolish its entire military organization, lock, stock, and barrel.'

Again, notwithstanding his antipathy against socialism and democracy (as he understood or mis-

---

[1] *Human All-Too-Human,* vol. ii—" The Wanderer and His Shadow," § 284 (p. 336 f.).

understood them) Nietzsche nevertheless noted with warm approval the tendency of these movements to remove national enmities, to promote the comity of nations, and to direct all the energies and resources of mankind into the right channels. He explained that the common fear of socialism prompts all political powers to flatter the masses, and to grant them all kinds of facilities and liberties. Eventually, he thought, the masses will become omnipotent, and the practical outcome of the increasing democratization will be a European league of nations, in which each nation will have the position of a canton with its separate rights. A certain re-adjustment of frontiers will be necessary in the best interests both of the several cantons and of the federation as a whole. Statesmanship will undergo a corresponding transformation. A new order of statesmen will arise—statesmen who will have made a special study of the arts and sciences of civilization, and who will put their trust, not in armies, but in moral motives and social utilities. Home politics will cease to be the Cinderella of foreign politics : the two will be inseparably connected for the good of each and all.[1] Nietzsche even ventured the prophecy that some

[1] *Human All-Too-Human,* vol. i, § 292 (p. 343 f.).

day education will be mainly directed to the establishment of a political policy for humanity as a whole.[1]

Now, one may or may not agree with these views of Nietzsche's. To some people, even to such as feel no special sympathy with present-day Germany, his criticisms may appear exaggerated. Anyhow, if Nietzsche erred, he certainly did not err in favour of chauvinism in general, or of Teutomania in particular. His political views remind one of the peace societies and of the Society of Friends rather than of Bernhardi and Treitschke.

How, then, it may well be asked, has it come about that the name of Nietzsche has become so prominently associated, in the public mind, with the names of the most notorious advocates of Teutomania?

The reason is this. Any system of ethics that is characterized by naturalism and evolutionism lends itself readily to the kind of glorification of struggle, war and victory, that gives a certain specious support to the cause of militarism and jingoism. And Nietzsche's writings not only present such an ethics of naturalism and evolutionism, they also present it in a manner which played into the hands of mili-

---

[1] *The Will to Power*, vol. ii, § 1057 (p. 423).

tarists and jingoes. His weakness for epigram and paradox too often betrayed him into utterances the playful extravagance of which was rather obscured by the unsystematic form of his writing. It was, therefore, perfectly easy to dress up the chauvinists' poverty of thought in the brilliant raiment of Nietzsche's picturesque language. And it is the frequent association of Nietzschean phrases with Teutomaniac ideas that has given rise to the popular view of Nietzsche's relation to the present war. But the view is incorrect and unjust. Teutomania, as I have already shown, was very far from Nietzsche's heart and soul. It is the Prussian jingo's heart wrapped in Nietzsche's skin.

The real views of Nietzsche and their remoteness from their bellicose distortions will become still clearer when his philosophy has been explained. It may, however, be as well to point out now one or two instances of the simplest kind of misinterpretation due to a disregard, not only of Nietzsche's whole trend of thought, but even of the immediate context of the dicta in question.

Bernhardi has adopted as the motto of his war-cry, *Germany and the Next War,* Nietzsche's dictum that " war and courage have done more great things than the love of one's neighbour."

Even more notorious has become the dictum, " ye say that it is the good cause that halloweth even war? I say unto you : it is the good war that halloweth any cause." Now both these murderous-sounding dicta occur in the same passage in *Thus spake Zarathustra*,[1] and a careful reading of the context shows that what Nietzsche is really speaking about is the war of ideas. Here are some of the sentences which precede the dicta under discussion : " If ye cannot be saints of knowledge, then, I pray you, be at least its warriors. . . . Your war shall ye wage for the sake of your thoughts! And if your thought succumb, yet will your uprightness proclaim its triumph!" The same is true of yet another famous war-dictum : " The man who has renounced war has renounced a grand life." Nietzsche, it should be remembered, was not a professional soldier, but a thinker and an ardent student of Greek philosophy. To him the term " war " did not primarily suggest battlefields, but something quite different. He thought of it in that comprehensive or attenuated sense in which it was used by Heraclitus, for whom Nietzsche felt the warmest admiration, and whose philosophy suggested to Nietzsche so much of his

[1] Part I.—Chapter on " War and Warriors," (p. 52).

own philosophy. In any case it is safe to assert that as a general rule when Nietzsche speaks of " war " he means the interplay of cosmic forces, or the struggle of ideas, or opposition to oppressive conventions, or the struggle with one's own passions and impulses to secure self-mastery. As already remarked, he does sometimes speak of real war as a drastic cure for national decadence. But he does not commend it as something good in itself, and he even points out with satisfaction other means, or effective substitutes for war, whereby national energy may be maintained, and the natural war instincts of man satisfied. The Roman substitutes for war consisted of " gladiatorial combats and persecutions of Christians." The English have done better. They have taken to mountaineering, seamanship, and dangerous exploring expeditions. Nietzsche thinks that " many such substitutes for war will be discovered."[1]

Much as Nietzsche loved bravery he must be acquitted of the charge that he commended warfare for its own sake. He fully realized that there are enough, and more than enough opportunities for the exercise of courage in the arts and pursuits of peace. And he rather suspected that an uncon-

[1] *Human All-Too-Human*, vol. i, § 477 (p. 349 f.).

scious shirking of their usual work in peace time has something to do with the enthusiasm of civilians whenever war breaks out. Their noble rush to the colours may, according to Nietzsche, be influenced by the unconscious desire to get away from their work and work-a-day world. In some cases war may, again unconsciously perhaps, be " a detour to suicide, a detour with a good conscience."[1] This may sound cynical, though I do not think he meant it cynically. At all events, it is not the language of a fire-brand. No! Nietzsche had seen war in all its grimness, and he had no illusions about it. Moreover, he was no monster. He could, and did, endure much suffering unflinchingly. But he had no perverted taste for unnecessary cruelty and slaughter. " There are," he said, " enough sublime things without its being necessary to seek sublimity where it is linked with cruelty; my ambition would not be gratified in the least if I aspired to be a sublime executioner."[2]

[1] *Joyful Wisdom*, § 338 (p. 268).
[2] *Ibid*, § 313 (p. 245).

CHAPTER II

I HAVE dwelt at some length on Nietzsche's alleged responsibility for that bellicose trend of German thought which has helped to precipitate the present war. I have done so partly because the question has an intrinsic interest; partly because it also brings to light an integral part of his social or political philosophy; but chiefly because it may serve as a useful warning that the prevailing views on Nietzsche must not be accepted uncritically.

Nietzsche once complained that what we do is sometimes praised, and sometimes blamed, but never understood. Allowing for a certain amount of exaggeration, the remark is peculiarly true of his own writings. It would be no grave injustice to assert that most of the usual accounts of his thought are, in some respects at least, misrepresentations of it.

It is highly probable that some of these misrepresentations of Nietzsche's views have done no little mischief in encouraging megalomania and other evils. But is it reasonable to hold anyone responsible, not only for his real views, but also for other people's distortions of them? I for one would protest against such severity. So would all teachers—and especially those of them who have had occasion to examine their own students. Some people seem to be specially gifted with the power of misapprehension : it appears to be the one way in which their originality expresses itself. Besides, if the absurd and evil consequences brought about by the misrepresentations of any cause were to be regarded as vitiating it, what philosophy, what religion, what other human venture would stand uncondemned?

It is unfortunately extremely easy to misunderstand Nietzsche; it requires no special gifts. His literary manner, and his philosophical method, or want of method, present peculiar pitfalls to the unwary. For a long time, in fact for the greatest part of his active career, he was addressing a deaf world. And who does not know how difficult it is to speak to the deaf in accents sweet and low? How many people, under such circumstances, do not succumb to the temptation to shout, to exaggerate their manner of speaking, and thereby also the matter of their speech? We also know, and Nietzsche knew only too well, the power of paradox to attract the attention of some clever people.[1] Moreover, he was an artist by temperament, and just revelled in the sheer skill of plastic literary expression. The result is a wealth of trenchant epigrams and an abundance of pregnant aphorisms which the superficial may readily use as a kind of philosophical spice to be taken, a grain or two at a time, to stimulate jaded nerves. And so numerous and varied are his aphorisms that almost anybody may seek there what he wants, and find what he seeks. Aristocrats and radicals, the dainty and the bully, the militarist and the pacifist, optimists and pessimists, saints and sinners—they can one and all find suitable texts in the writings of Nietzsche, provided they are not too nice about his real meaning and the true drift of his philosophy as a whole. This proviso is unfortunately only too easy to fulfil. The greater part of his writings consists of texts rather than of continuous discourses; and texts, even the most sacred texts, are liable to all kinds of interpretations and misinterpretations to suit the individual tastes of the interpreter. No doubt aphorisms have a charm of

[1] Compare Mr. Shaw's candid confession : " In this world, if you do not say a thing in an irritating way, you may just as well not say it at all, since nobody will trouble themselves about anything which does not trouble them."

their own; they stimulate the mind of the reader to help to bring to birth the pregnant text. But the meaning read into it by the reader is not always the meaning of the author, who thus has fathered upon him children that are not his own.

There were special reasons why Nietzsche expressed his thoughts for the most part in the dogmatic and unsystematic form of the aphorism. Originally this form of literary expression appears to have been forced upon him by his ill-health, which made prolonged application impossible. But in course of time he found it congenial, and saw good reasons for going on with it. One reason is to be found in his belief that most people are more impressed by confident, dogmatic assertions than by long, reasoned arguments.[1] Another reason may be found in a certain literary conceit of Nietzsche's—it was his ambition, he confesses, " to say in ten sentences what everyone else says in a whole book; what everyone else does *not* say even in a whole book."[2] There is yet another and much deeper reason, which it will be more convenient to explain when I come to state his views on the mind of man. But in any case it would be

---

[1] *Human All-Too-Human*, vol. ii, § 295 (p. 142).
[2] *The Twilight of the Idols*—" Skirmishes," etc., § 51 (p. 111).

rash to conclude that brevity of expression is evidence of insufficient consideration. " In spite of its embryonic appearance," says Nietzsche, " a brief dictum may be the fruit of long reflection."

There is yet another difficulty in the path of the inquirer who looks for a coherent philosophy in Nietzsche's writings. Not only is it undeniable that Nietzsche's views underwent appreciable changes as the years rolled on, but he almost seems to boast of his " short-lived habits " in modes of thought as well as in other matters. A periodical change of views appeared to him to be a vital necessity to mental alertness. " The snake that cannot cast its skin perishes. So, too, with those minds which are prevented from changing their views : they cease to be minds."[1] It was for this reason probably that he had no faith in philosophical systems and systematizers. " The will to a system (he suggests) shows a lack of honesty,"[2] apparently because by the time one's views have been elaborated into a system they are already changing, and one is tempted to cling to the system from vanity and pride. Lastly, out of his own mouth Nietzsche seems to condemn himself and his

[1] *The Dawn of Day*, § 573 (p. 394).
[2] *The Twilight of the Idols*—" Maxims," § 26 (p. 5).

philosophy when, near the end of his literary activity, he confesses : " Heretofore I have been a nihilist from top to toe."[1]

In view of all this, it is perhaps not altogether unnatural that some people should decline to describe Nietzsche as a philosopher at all, and should look upon him rather as a brilliant *littérateur* and eccentric free lance, an incarnation of the spirit that ever denies, always prone to contradict everything and everybody—even himself! Some even profess to see in his writings little more than mad extravagances, ominous forebodings of the tragic fate which eventually overtook him. Now, Nietzsche's writings are certainly not entirely free from eccentricity, but they by no means bear out the above charge. For the rest, his self-criticism must be received with as much caution as his self-praise. His views should be treated on their own merits, and not prejudged on account of his subsequent insanity.

Some critics, not content with some such sweeping indictment of Nietzsche as was indicated above, promptly proceed to dismember his speculations into their component ideas, and to trace these to various preceding thinkers. Heraclitus and the

---

[1] *The Will to Power*, vol. i, § 25 (p. 22).

Sophists, Plato and the Cynics, Spinoza and Leibniz, Kant and Schopenhauer, Darwin and Spencer, not to mention others, are credited with numerous contributions to Nietzsche's philosophy. Now, it is quite true, I think, that he was indebted to all these for all sorts of important suggestions. The extraordinary originality which enthusiastic Nietzscheites find in his writings is mainly due to their own unfamiliarity with the history of philosophy. But, anyhow, those who have seriously tried to understand, I will not say all, but even one or two only of the philosophers on whom Nietzsche has drawn, will realize that it requires more than ordinary sanity and insight in order to acquire a working knowledge of them. And Nietzsche's writings beyond a doubt show a very considerable knowledge of the history of philosophy, both ancient and modern—enough and more than enough to render utterly absurd any perfunctory attempt to dismiss them as the irresponsible utterances of a madman. Moreover, he does show some originality in his use of the old material—as will appear from the account of his philosophy which will be given presently.

The fact is that to understand Nietzsche he must be studied with more than usual care, while his style appears to invite, on the contrary, the most casual reading.   At first sight, it appears to matter little, if at all, which volume of aphorisms is read first, or whether the contents of any one volume are read forwards or backwards.   But that is not the way to get an insight into his thought.   He requires more painstaking care than does a systematic writer.   A systematic writer may be understood correctly, if not completely, even if only one of his books has been read.   But Nietzsche's writings must be read through almost from beginning to end, and in their chronological sequence, if one is to carry away a correct impression even of the main drift of his thought.   The student of Nietzsche must, in fact, take upon himself the onerous function of a philosophical executor or editor, and do for him what Nietzsche would have done for himself if he had only been spared a little longer.   After all, Nietzsche was only forty-four years old when his career as a thinker and writer came to a premature end.   And there is good reason to believe that it was his intention ultimately to express his philosophy in systematic form, notwithstanding his earlier aversion to systems.   I do not mean to say that it is worth everybody's while to take such pains with Nietzsche.   Far from it. But I do say that, until one has studied him with such care, one may praise him, or one may blame him, but one does not know him.

The unsystematic form of his writings will probably debar Nietzsche from ever holding a high place in the history of philosophy, but there is no doubt in my mind that he will have some place in it. That his claim to such a place should be disputed by some is nothing unusual. His case is one of those border cases which always give rise to such pedantic disputes. Every department of science and of art sooner or later brings one face to face with one or other of the problems of philosophy, if the questions pertaining to that department are only pushed far enough. And in almost every such department there are some few men for whom those border problems have a special fascination. Such amphibious inquirers are liable to be regarded with some uncertainty, if not with suspicion. There are eminent men whom mathematicians or physicists, or biologists, as the case may be, call philosophers, while philosophers call them mathematicians, or physicists, or biologists. And so it is also in the realm of poetry or of literature generally. Lessing and Goethe, Browning and Tennyson, are cases in point. Nietzsche's claim to a place in the history of philosophy is greater than theirs, it is even greater than that of Rousseau or of Carlyle, even if it is not quite so indisputable as in the case of Lucretius. Personally I have no faith in hard and fast lines of demarcation, and I do not believe that any such pedantry will ever exclude Nietzsche from his place in the honourable company of philosophers.

In some respects it is a great pity that Nietzsche never had to teach philosophy to students. Not that it is an unmitigated evil not to have to prepare undergraduates for examinations. But it would have compelled him to express himself more systematically and less ambiguously. As it is his writings are not exactly the safest books to put indiscriminately into everybody's hands. But that need not affect his position as a philosopher. Spiders, and even others, will gather poison where bees gather honey.

In what follows I propose to sketch the broad outlines of Nietzsche's philosophy, its motives and its results. It is neither possible, nor perhaps even desirable, that I should enter into great detail, or that I should indulge in much criticism, on the present occasion. But I hope to say enough to convey an adequate idea of the real philosophy of Nietzsche.

CHAPTER III

THE MOTIVE OF NIETZSCHE'S PHILOSOPHY

WHAT set Nietzsche on his philosophical inquiries was a feeling of profound discontent with the current conceptions of human life and destiny. He had come under conflicting influences. On the one hand, there was the austere conventionalism of his early environment, more especially his orthodox Christian home. On the other hand, there was the freer, more bracing atmosphere of classical paganism, which he breathed as an ardent student of classical literature, and future Professor of classical philology. The Greek view of life somehow appealed to him irresistibly. So that from the very first he felt himself to be " the nursling of older ages like the Greek " rather than a child of his own age;[1] and to the very last he looked upon the Greeks as " the highest type of men ever evolved hitherto.'"[2]

The conflict between the Christian and the Greek

---

[1] *Thoughts out of Season*, vol. ii, preface (p. 5).
[2] *The Will to Power*, vol. i, § 419 (p. 336).

views of life is an old one. And the Renaissance bears eloquent witness to the fascination which Greek culture can have for Christian minds. But even the Renaissance was a striking climax rather than a beginning of European resistance to certain Christian tendencies.

The tendency of early and mediæval Christianity was to deny or renounce the world and the flesh. Earthly life was looked upon as a kind of purgatory, an incessant conflict with unholy desires and evil spirits. The good Christian living the religious life tried to withdraw his eyes from all that is earthly, in order to fix his gaze on heaven, until the desires of the flesh perished, and his soul became rapt in mystical ecstasy. But such saintliness proved too much for human nature. *Naturam expellas furca, tamen usque recurret.* Man's primitive instincts re-asserted themselves in all kinds of ways, even before the advent of the Renaissance. Human nature found expression in the love-songs of the Troubadours, in the poetry of Boccaccio, and even in the divine Epic of Dante, whose adoration of Beatrice is a blending of sacred and profane love. But, of course, the Renaissance stands out as the great triumph of "Humanism," achieved by the aid of Greek inspiration. And

from the days of the Renaissance till the time of
Goethe and of Matthew Arnold, and, indeed, to
the present day, the study of Greek and Latin
literature has exercised an extraordinary fascination on the minds of many brilliant people, so that
they recoil from the oppressiveness of the ordinary
outlook on life and reality and show their prefer-
ence for a freer and more expansive culture like
that of classical paganism.

In some respects the antithesis between Greek
(or Pagan) and Christian just explained, is rather
unfortunate. It is really much exaggerated. In
practice, at all events, Christianity was never pure
renunciation or asceticism, nor was Hellenism pure
naturalism or freedom. Why, the very name
"asceticism" is of Greek origin. The contrast
really intended by the Greek view of life *versus*
the Christian, is a contrast which is met with *within*
each creed and people; and it is a pity that the so-
called Hellenic tendency should be represented as
anti-Christian, or anti-Hebraic. For the inmost
meaning of the tendency only becomes obscured
thereby, and its name only helps to swell the multi-
tude of misleading shibboleths.

The movement represented by the Renaissance,
and since then by such "pagans" as Goethe and

others, is only one form of an older and more comprehensive tendency already to be met with in ancient as well as in modern times. It is the tendency labelled with the familiar motto of " life according to nature," or " return to nature." The cry " return to nature," or "live according to nature," recurs again and again in the history of man. Ancient Sophists and Stoics advocated the life according to nature; even the Gospels demand a return to a childish state of nature as a condition of admission into heaven; in modern times Rousseau was the great prophet of nature; poets like Goethe and Wordsworth, and preachers like Tolstoy and Maeterlinck have echoed the call to follow nature; while cranks without number have devised all sorts of elaborate schemes for living the simple life. A cry taken up by people so unlike one another must needs be elastic and ambiguous. But on the other hand it could hardly have been taken up so frequently unless it somehow appealed to something deep-seated in human nature.

What, then, is the meaning of this cry, or this movement, and wherein lies its charm for so many?

As already suggested, it does not always mean quite the same things; parts of its meaning in one case may be different from, and even directly opposed to, parts of its meaning in another case. But one part of its significance is always this : it is a movement towards the liberation of the individual from the shackles of external authority, excessive conventionalism, and a fearful other-worldliness.

This kind of revolt lies ever near to the heart of a live and vigorous generation, desirous of shaping its own life and destiny, and unwilling to be mere clay in the hands of others, be they never so old and wise.   Rousseau has gained immortal fame as the herald of one such revolt, which culminated in the French Revolution. Nietzsche is the standard-bearer of another, the latest,and perhaps greatest, of these chronic revolts.   But, except in this respect, Nietzsche is about as unlike the sentimental Rousseau as anyone well can be.   And Nietzsche's popularity with so many people is mainly due to the fact that he voices their resentment against all that is hostile to spontaneous individuality, against all that tends to reduce mankind to the monotonous, lifeless uniformity of machine-made articles.

The central problem and goal of Nietzsche's reflections was, therefore, the problem of life and conduct, the ethical or moral problem.

This was the motive of his whole philosophy.
Nietzsche, however, realized very early in his
career that to *preach* a morality is a very different thing from *establishing* it.   And he was
determined to be a philosopher, not a preacher. He
was resolved to discover and establish new values
for life, not merely to propagate traditional ones.
And he saw clearly that the problem of life and
conduct, that is to say the properly ethical problem, cannot be divorced from the metaphysical
problems concerning the nature and validity of
human knowledge, and the nature of the universe.
In one of his earlier essays already he took David
Strauss severely to task for "constructing his
ethics quite independently of the question, 'What
is our conception of the universe?' "[1]

Nietzsche was determined, moreover, to be ex-
ceptionally thorough and searching in his inquiry
into the moral problem—not only more thorough
than a liberal theologian like Strauss, but more
thorough even than most professed philosophers
had been hitherto. It is, of course, of the very
essence of philosophy not to depend on tradition
or authority, but to seek an independent solution
of all the great problems of life and reality, and

[1] *Thoughts out of Season*, vol. i, " David Strauss," § vii (p. 50).

to exercise ruthless criticism in the estimation of every belief. Nietzsche complains, however, that the criticism and cross-examination have not been as searching as might be, especially in the domain of ethics. Liberal Christians, who had consigned all other Christian doctrines to the limbo of footless fancies, still identified Christianity with Christian ethics, which they accepted uncritically as something beyond the shadow of a doubt. And even the "critical" philosophers have not questioned the validity of Christian morality, but have accepted it as something "given" once for all, and have only sought to justify it, instead of criticizing it. "I see no one who has ventured to *criticize* the estimates of moral worth . . . With difficulty I have discovered some scanty data for the purpose of furnishing a *history of the origin* of these feelings and estimates of value, which is something different from a criticism of them . . . There is little to be learned from the historians of morality . . . they themselves are usually, quite unsuspectingly, under the influence of a definite morality, and unwittingly act as its armour-bearers or followers . . . No one has hitherto tested the *value* of morality : for which purpose it is first of all necessary for someone to call it in question.

Well, that is just our work."[1]   And Nietzsche did this work so thoroughly that he could rightly claim that nobody else had ever "looked at the world with such a profound suspicion."[2] His un-compromising honesty is one of the things that make his views so stimulating even, or perhaps especially, to those who do not agree with him. He nothing attenuates, nor sets down aught in malice.

In conformity with his views on the intimate connection between ethics and metaphysics, Nietzsche devoted considerable attention to problems of knowledge and reality. Accordingly, before turning to his views on life and conduct, I propose to outline, in the next two chapters, his theory of knowledge, and his views on the ultimate nature of the universe. These parts of his philosophy are much more important for the understanding of Nietzsche than one would gather from the popular expositions of his thought. They are, moreover, highly interesting, and anticipate a good many doctrines that have since his time become more or less familiar in connection with Pragmatism, Humanism, and the Philosphy of Creative Evolution.

---

[1] *Joyful Wisdom,* § 345 (p. 281), *cf. Beyond Good and Evil,* § 186 (p. 103 f.).

[2] *Human All-Too-Human,* vol. i, preface, § 1 (p. 1).

CHAPTER IV

NIETZSCHE'S THEORY OF KNOWLEDGE

IN this chapter and the next we have to consider
the most difficult parts of Nietzsche's philosophy,
namely, his views on the nature and validity of
human knowledge, and his views on the ultimate
constitution of the universe. These are problems
which it is always difficult to treat separately.
They are so intimately connected. Our views
regarding human knowledge are bound to affect
our conception of reality, and conversely our conception of the ultimate nature of reality is bound
to involve certain assumptions in relation to human
knowledge. At best each group of topics can only
be discussed separately on the basis of certain
explicit assumptions provisionally made with reference to the other group of topics. And that is
what is usually done by systematic writers in order
to prevent, as far as may be, the bewildering tangle
which inevitably results when all problems are
attacked at once. Now Nietzsche makes no attempt to group his problems, or to discuss them in

any kind of logical sequence. Problems of knowledge and problems of reality, questions of the greatest importance and questions of the smallest importance—to say nothing of more or less flippant remarks—follow each other with mutual unconcern. His spirit bloweth where it listeth. This, of course, aggravates the difficulties of the serious student or exponent of Nietzsche's philosophy. He must do for Nietzsche what every author is expected to do for himself, namely, arrange and systematize and generally edit his utterances. Still, the broad outlines of Nietzsche's thought on the chief problems of philosophy are clear enough to the careful reader. The chief difficulty is presented by the occurrence of different views on the same subject, not only in different books, but sometimes even in the same book. This difficulty too, however, is not insuperable. Sometimes the difference is clearly due to a change of view, and as a rule it is possible to determine which was his final opinion. In other cases we simply have various suggestions which, though incompatible, probably appeared to him to be more or less equally plausible, so that he could not decide between them. Instead of merely ignoring such hypotheses as did not fit into his general scheme, or were

D

not consistent with what he had already said, he is honest enough to put down whatever occurred to him as a possible solution of the problem. This is what makes people accuse him of the maddest inconsistency. But such people are simply deceived by his literary manner. His manner of *writing* is dogmatic—every suggestion is expressed as though it were gospel truth. But his manner of *thinking* is far removed from dogmatism. He frankly admits that he is not absolutely certain about anything. But that is no reason why he should not, to the best of his ability, try to form an independent opinion on each of the great problems of life and reality; and when several rival views appear to be equally plausible he states them all without prejudice. His dogmatic literary formulation of them is simply his manner of trying to do them justice in the way of forcible and persuasive expression. There can be no reasonable doubt that Nietzsche (like almost every other philosopher) regarded his views as no more than reasonable and helpful suggestions, not as established theories, or as sure dogmas. This will become clear from his theory of knowledge, to the consideration of which we may now proceed.

The first and most fundamental question that

confronts the critical philosopher is, "Is there such a thing as human knowledge at all?" Usually it is assumed as a matter of course that there is such a thing as knowledge : that men, indeed, do not know everything, far from it, but that we do know some things. But now, what do we mean when we speak of possessing knowledge of things? We mean that our minds entertain certain beliefs which represent certain things as they really are. In other words, it is commonly assumed that, on the one hand, there are human minds; that, on the other hand, there is an immense variety of things; that in the human mind there are beliefs relating to some of those things; and that the beliefs in the mind may, and often do, represent those things just as they are. So much is implied in the usual assumption that there is such a thing as human knowledge. But, it may be asked, what warranty is there for the accuracy of the assumption and its implications?

This fundamental problem is attacked by Nietzsche in a radical and interesting manner. In questioning the possibility of human knowledge, the human understanding (Nietzsche remarks) is really criticizing its own fitness to serve as an instrument of knowledge. And Nietzsche deems it beyond the range of probabilities for an instrument to criticize properly its own fitness.[1] Consider (he urges) what would be required in order to answer the question of human knowledge in a reiiable and decisive manner. It would require some sort of higher creature endowed with absolute knowledge, both of the things themselves and of our beliefs concerning them, in order to compare our beliefs on the one hand, with the things themselves on the other, and so determine their agreement or disagreement. Now, whether there are such higher creatures or not, we at all events do not know them, and we ourselves certainly cannot carry out the required comparison. We cannot step outside our own minds, and have a peep at things as they are in themselves, in order to compare our previous beliefs with the things themselves. We cannot, therefore, be really sure that we know reality or any part of it. We entertain beliefs, certainly; but whether our beliefs are true, who can say?[2]

Still, it may be urged, this is no proof that our beliefs are all erroneous. The fact that we cannot transcend our own minds and prove the accuracy

[1] *The Will to Power*, vol. i, § 410 (p. 329).
 Ibid., vol. ii, § 473 (p. 5 f.).

of our beliefs and modes of apprehension by comparing them with things as they are in themselves, still leaves it possible that we may have real knowledge, even though we cannot prove it in the manner suggested. Nietzsche, however, is inclined to suspect all so-called human knowledge. Employing the familiar argument that " knowing means to place oneself in relation to something known," he maintains sometimes that this very relationship makes it impossible for things to become known to us absolutely as they are in themselves; in becoming known they are conditioned by our knowing.[1] But, it may be urged again, may not this relationship between the knowing mind and known object be a transparent relationship—a relationship, that is to say, which does not affect the character of the thing known even as known? In other words, may not things be known just for what they are, in spite of the relationship of being known? May not, in fact, the whole distinction between things as they are in themselves and things as they are known be a gratuitous distinction as regards essentials?

Now, Nietzsche does, indeed, question the validity of the whole distinction. " We do not know enough " (he says) " to be entitled even to

[1] *The Will to Power*, vol. ii, § 555 (p. 64).

make such a distinction between ' thing-in-itself '
and 'phenomenon' '"; and sometimes he even cata-
gorically rejects " things-in-themselves.'"²   But,
on the whole, he thinks, with Kant and others,
that human knowledge is not a mere reflection, in
the mirror of the mind, of a reality outside it.
He thinks that the act of apprehension does not
leave what is apprehended in all its original naked-
ness, but clothes it, as it were, in swaddling clothes
supplied by the apprehending mind.   Or, to use
another metaphor, the human mind catches its
flies, not directly, but only by enmeshing them
first in cobwebs spun out of itself.   So that what
the mind grasps is, not the naked fly in itself, but
the fly wrapt up in, and obscured by, the cobwebs
of the apprehending mind.   In other words, the
mind is not " merely passive," it is a " creative
power "; it does not simply reflect things like a
mirror, but partly at least " creates " what it
" knows.'"³   " Perhaps," says Nietzsche, " man
ultimately only finds in things what he has put
into them.'"⁴   And he anticipates the Pragmatist
view that " ' Truth ' is not something which is

¹ *Joyful Wisdom*, § 354 (p. 300).
² *The Will to Power*, vol. ii, § 555 (p. 64).
³ *Ibid*, § 673 (p. 144).
⁴ *Ibid*, § 606 (p. 103).

already there to be found or discovered; it is something which has to be created.'" Our so-called " truths," in short, are " man-made."

If so, then there may be no such thing as real human knowledge, but only human error. Even the most general beliefs of mankind, and our common ways of regarding the world of reality, may all be false, mere figments of the imagination. Such universal assumptions as that there are enduring " things," things of the same " kind," " causes," and " effects," etc., etc., may all be mere fictions. All the categories of common sense and of science may be so many ways of veiling reality, rather than of revealing it. Verily, truth may lie at the bottom of the well, where, foiled by his own reflection, man looks for her in vain.

But, it may be protested again, does not the very survival of certain beliefs, and of the people who entertain them, show that they are true? Does not the fact that we are often compelled to repudiate some beliefs, because of their incompatibility with reality, show that those beliefs which we do retain, and which help us to cope with the world successfully, are true, or at least are not all false? Nietzsche's reply is as follows: The view

¹ *The Will to Power*, vol. ii, § 552 (p. 60).

that all our beliefs and ways of regarding things
are alike untrue, does not mean that they are all
alike in every respect—that they are all equally
worthless. Not at all. Some beliefs and ways of
regarding the world happen to be helpful to life,
others are injurious to life. Those members or
varieties of the human species who entertained injurious beliefs perished in course of time, and with
them perished those beliefs. On the other hand,
those who happened to hit on useful beliefs—that
is to say, life-preserving beliefs and ways of regarding reality—survived and transmitted them to
their offspring, with the result that these useful
beliefs have become the common stock of mankind.
But even these beliefs are erroneous all the same—
they are " useful," but not " true." In fact, the
proper distinction is, not between " truths " and
" errors," but between " useful errors " and
" errors that are not useful." For " utility "
(Nietzsche insists) is not " truth," and although it
is conceivable that beliefs may be useful because
they are true, yet they may be useful even if they
are not true, perhaps even because they are not
true. " Our trust in reason and its categories,"
says Nietzsche, " proves only that experience has
taught the *usefulness* of these things to life; not

their truth.'" The human mind, in short, may only be " an instrument of power," that is, of life, and not an instrument for the discovery of "truth." The logical and mathematical notions and the methods of common sense and of science are just the result of " our attempt to make the actual world more calculable, and more susceptible to formulation, for our own purposes.'" Take, for instance, the notions of "substance " (or "thing"), " cause " and " effect." Reality may be a continuum, an incessant flux of processes which only *appear* to us as separate " things," " causes " and " effects," simply because our powers of perception are too coarse to apprehend the infinite subtlety of the endless flow of reality, or because such an apprehension would be too bewildering for human life. And so we break up the continuous flow of events into separate " things," we subsume them under "mummified concepts.'"and, projecting into them our feelings of strength, we regard some of them as " causes " producing others as their " effects.'" But all this, says Nietzsche, is sheer " humanizing " (*Anmenschlichung*). In

---

[1] *The Will to Power*, vol. ii, § 507 (p. 26).
[2] *Ibid.*, § 516 (p. 33).
[3] *The Twilight of the Idols*—" Reason in Philosophy," § 1 (p. 17).
[4] *The Will to Power*, vol. ii, § 664 (p. 136 f.).

fact all "knowledge" and all "science" consists of
such "humanizing" methods and results[1]—that is to
say, ways of regarding and treating reality so as to
suit the convenience of man and his peculiar make
up.   And the human way of regarding the world
and the fulness thereof may be but " one idiosyncrasy among many others."[2]   Anyhow, what is
humanly convenient is not necessarily true.   Indeed, why should we suppose that the needs of
human life cannot be sufficiently served by anything short of the truth, or even by something very
different from it?   " Suppose," says Nietzsche,
" that man is just not the measure of things."[3]
" A thing might be *true* even if it is injurious or
dangerous in the highest degree ; indeed, the essential constitution of reality might be such that a full
knowledge of it might prove fatal," so that the
truth would have to be " veiled, sugared, falsi-
fied " in order to make it endurable, that is to say,
in order to make life possible.[4]

For mankind, of course, such helpful life-sus-
taining beliefs are of supreme importance even if
they be erroneous.   What, forsooth, could be more

[1] *Joyful Wisdom*, § 112 (p. 158).
[2] *The Will to Power*, vol. ii, § 515 (p. 30).
[3] *Beyond Good and Evil*, § 3 (p. 8).
[4] *Ibid.*, § 39 (p. 53 f.).

important for man than the preservation of the species? These useful errors must, therefore, by no means be despised. Indeed, if one is helped to appreciate their value better by calling them "truths," there is no harm in that—provided it is borne in mind that our standpoint is merely "anthropocentric," and that we do not set up human idiosyncrasy as the final measure of reality.[1] It is interesting to observe that Nietzsche, unlike some subsequent "humanists," does not hold that "useful beliefs" are really truths, and all that people mean by "truths." He was not quite so eccentric as that.

But, it may be asked, can we not pass beyond mere human idiosyncrasy? Can we not transcend the merely human standpoint? May not our very realization of the utilitarian and anthropocentric character of human reason and its categories enable us to rise above them to a higher and truer point of view? No, thinks Nietzsche. What happens here is very like what happens in the familiar phenomena of perspective. We may "know" that the picture before our eyes is flat, is in one plane only, and yet on looking at it we cannot help "seeing" three dimensions. We cannot help it, we are

[1] *The Will to Power*, vol. ii, § 584 (p. 85).

made to see such things in that way.   In the same
way even the philosopher who has reflected on the
"humanism" of human knowledge, cannot liberate
himself from the human perspective.   " We cannot," says Nietzsche, " see round our corner : it is
hopeless curiosity to want to know what other
modes of intellect and perspective there might be :
for example, whether any kind of being could per-
ceive time backwards, or alternately forwards and
backwards, whereby another direction of life and
another conception of cause and effect would be
given."   But, of course, " we cannot dismiss the
possibility that the world contains infinite interpretations " and perspectives.[1]

Such are the most salient points in Nietzsche's
theory of knowledge.   Other interesting views
connected with his theory of knowledge will be
dealt with more conveniently in the chapters which
follow.

Even this bare outline of Nietzsche's theory of
knowledge has probably made it sufficiently clear

---

[1] *Joyful Wisdom,* § 374 (p. 341).—Nietzsche's anticipation of
" another conception of cause and effect " has been fulfilled.   Mr.
Bertrand Russell writes : " It is customary only to give the name
' effect ' to an event which is later than the cause, but there is
no kind of reason for this restriction.   We shall do better to allow
the effect to be before the cause or simultaneous with it, because
nothing of any scientific importance depends upon its being after
the cause."—*Our Knowledge of the External World* (p. 226).

that it is not at all conducive to dogmatism or to over-confidence in one's opinions. That is what I had in my mind, when I insisted, at the commencement of the present chapter, that, notwithstanding his literary manner, it would be a mistake to suppose that Nietzsche was really dogmatic or over-confident in his views.

But if Nietzsche was not a dogmatist, he was also not merely a sceptic, as some say he was. In fact, he held the sceptical attitude in very low esteem. "Scepticism," he said, "is a result of decadence."[1] It is "the most spiritual expression of . . . nervous debility and sickliness."[2] Nietzsche was extremely critical rather than sceptical. The main point of his theory of knowledge, I take it, was to bring out the human "perspective" involved in all human "knowledge"—somewhat as Kant and others had done before him, only more so. We have seen already that he did not dismiss all opinions as equally worthless. Far from it. He valued human thought highly as a potent factor in shaping life and reality. Strange as it may appear at first sight, he even approved martyrdom in the cause of one's views. "We should not,"

---

[1] *The Will to Power*, vol. i, § 43 (p. 34).
[2] *Beyond Good and Evil*, § 208 (p. 144).

he said, "let ourselves be burnt for our opinions—
we are not so sure of them as all that. But," he
carefully added, "we might well let ourselves be
burnt for the right of holding and changing our
opinions."[1]

Taken as a whole, Nietzsche's theory of knowledge is certainly not particularly cheerful. One
is inclined to suggest that even allowing for all
his criticisms of human knowledge the final result
might perhaps have been somewhat more sanguine
than it appears to be. When explaining his views
I indicated in one or two places that his criticisms
only tend to show that the validity of human knowledge cannot be *proved* in the way in which he
wanted it proved. But—even if we waive the
question whether his conception of the ultimate
test of human knowledge be the only one admis-
sible—it might have been pointed out by Nietzsche
that *not to prove* is not yet the same as to *disprove*.
Consequently, even if we allow that he has succeeded in showing that the validity of human
knowledge *cannot be proved*, at all events he has
not *disproved* it. Human knowledge is, therefore,
still *possible*, though not proved to be certain, in
the way in which Nietzsche wanted it proved.

[1] *Human All-Too-Human*, vol. ii, § 333 (p. 358).

Moreover, even if we grant, as, indeed, we may
grant, his principal contention, namely, that our
so-called knowledge is only the peculiar way in
which the world appears in *human perspective*,
still man, and therefore the human perspective,
is real enough. Consequently human knowledge,
so long as we remember that it is human, is true
as far as it goes, even if it is not the whole truth.

Explicitly, however, Nietzsche appears to make
little or nothing of these possibilities. He seems
to accept with alacrity the more cheerless alternative, namely, that for man there is probably no
real truth or knowledge. Something more will
be said on this head in the next chapter. But
what I particularly wish to draw attention to now
is a certain pessimistic bias in Nietzsche's mental
make-up. The most cheerless alternative seems
to fascinate him most. I do not mean to suggest
that Nietzsche was a pessimist, as so many people
think he was. He was a pessimist only for a short
time in the early part of his career, when he was
still under the dominant influence of Schopenhauer. But he soon got over that—curiously
enough, it was his illness that cured him of his
pessimism. And for the rest of his active life he
not only dropped pessimism, but strongly opposed

it. Nevertheless, the ghost of his former pessimism seems to haunt him constantly, and to incline him in favour of the least cheerful possibilities. True, this may help to bring his courage into greater relief : the more cheerless the outlook, the greater is the courage required to assent to it, to say "yea" to it cheerfully. But in an impartial survey of knowledge and reality, such a pessimistic bias has no special virtue, and must be taken into account when studying Nietzsche.

CHAPTER V

NIETZSCHE'S theory of knowledge, as sketched in the preceding chapter, does not appear to offer any real basis for further philosophical construction. And one is curious to know what kind of a theory of the universe, or philosophy of nature, he can base upon it. Some may be surprised that Nietzsche should have formulated a view of the world at all : they may think that he should have confessed his agnosticism and abandoned all attempts at a cosmology. Some writers, indeed, pay little heed to his theory of knowledge or his theory of the universe, and confine themselves to an exposition of his views on man and superman. Such a method is certainly convenient, but, as Nietzsche has rightly insisted, what is convenient is not necessarily correct.

Nietzsche has a cosmology, or theory of the universe, just as he has an epistemology, or theory of knowledge. He treats them both most seriously as integral parts of his philosophy, which is only caricatured by their omission.

E

The fact is that Nietzsche's theory of knowledge is not quite so drastic or agnostic as it appears to be at the first blush. I have already suggested, in the preceding chapter, that one may grant Nietzsche's contention about the human perspective entering into human knowledge, and yet maintain that our "knowledge" is true, even if it is not the whole truth : in other words, that reality in its relation to man really is what it appears to be, that the world in human perspective really is what we take it to be, although it may also be, and appear to be, different in other than human perspectives, that is, to other beings than ourselves. Such a view virtually allows the validity of human knowledge, so long as it is recognized as human. Now, to my mind, that is really Nietzsche's view, the view that he implicitly relies upon and builds on, even if he does not state and admit it explicitly. The real significance of what he calls *Perspektivismus*, or the "perspective" theory of knowledge, is apt to be obscured by the fact that he is constantly repudiating the possibility of "knowledge," and insisting that we are confined to mere "appearance" and "illusion" (*Schein*). But what he means by "knowledge" is some hypothetical, absolute knowledge guaranteed to represent its objects just as they are, and unaffected in any way by their relation to the knowing subject. Now, who could undertake to prove or to guarantee all that? Still, the refusal to do all that, is quite compatible with such recognition of the validity of human knowledge as I have just indicated, and which, I maintain, represents the real view of Nietzsche.

If so, then there is nothing inconsistent in Nietzsche's formulating a cosmology, and in his insisting upon the importance of our opinions in shaping human life and destiny, perhaps even in moulding to some extent the nature of the universe.

Now, the first question to be considered in a theory of the universe is that of its ultimate constitution. What is the world made of? Nietzsche's attempt to answer the question is guided by two principles :—

(1) only to posit such modes of being as we are most sure of in the way of actual experience; and

(2) not to assume more kinds of reality than is necessary to explain the world as we know it.

Now, what is it that we are surest of? Our

strivings, says Nietzsche, our instinctive impulses and cravings, these are the things of which
we are most sure by way of the most direct
experience.   That much, then, is " given," or
may be regarded as a datum for the construction
of a philosophy of nature.   Is there anything else
of which we are as sure?   Nothing else, according
to Nietzsche, seems to be " given " in the same
way.   Still this may suffice.   " Supposing," says
he, "that nothing else is 'given ' as real but our
world of desires and feelings, supposing that we
cannot get down to, or reach up to, any other
' reality ' but just that of our impulses . . . are
we not permitted to make the attempt and to ask
the question whether this which is ' given ' does
not *suffice* . . . for the understanding even of
the so-called mechanical (or ' material ') world?
I do not mean as an illusion, appearance, idea, or
Vorstellung (in the Berkeleyan and Schopenhauerian sense), but as possessing the same grade
of reality as our feelings themselves possess—a
more primitive form of the world of feelings, in
which all things are still locked in a mighty unity,
which afterwards differentiates and develops into
organic processes . . . a kind of instinctive life
in which all organic functions . . . are still fused

. . . a primitive form of life?   After all, such an attempt is not only allowed, but is demanded by logical method.   Not to assume several kinds of causality, so long as the attempt to get along with a single one has not been pushed to its furthest extent . . . is a rule of method which one may not repudiate nowadays."[1]

Nietzsche's view, then, of the ultimate constitution of reality may be stated somewhat as follows.   The centres of energy, by the aid of which the physicist would explain nature, are, according to Nietzsche, centres of impulse—centres, that is to say, which inwardly experience essentially the same kind of impulses as man experiences within himself, albeit the impulses or experiences vary enormously in degree of development. Even what appears to us, who can only look at it from the outside, as inert matter, is experienced or felt within itself as a kind of impulse, though an impulse of an extremely rudimentary or primitive kind.   Now impulse in its most developed form is commonly described as "will."   If the application of the term "will" be extended so as to cover all forms of impulse, from the lowest to the highest, then the world may be said to be a

[1] *Beyond Good and Evil*, § 36 (p. 51).

world of "will"—only it must be carefully borne in mind that in the lower forms of reality this "will" is never conscious, and that even in man it is for the most part unconscious or sub-conscious.

This essentially Schopenhauerian view of nature was one of the early links between Nietzsche and Wagner. Wagner's power of giving it musical expression was one of the principal causes of Nietzsche's early enthusiasm for him. In one of his earliest essays, Nietzsche wrote : " In general it may be said of Wagner, the musician, that he endowed everything in nature, which hitherto had had no wish to speak, with the power of speech. He refuses to admit that anything must be dumb, and, resorting to the dawn, the forest, the mist, the cliffs, the hills, the thrill of night, and the moonlight, he observes a desire common to them all—they too wish to sing their own melody. If the philosopher says it is will that struggles for existence in animate and inanimate nature, the musician adds : and this will, wherever it manifests itself, yearns for a melodious existence."[1]

But, to return to Nietzsche's conception of the world as "will." What, it may be asked, is the

---

[1] *Thoughts out of Season,* vol. i—" Richard Wagner in Bayreuth," § ix (p. 179 f.).

general tendency of the will or impulse which constitutes the universe? Nietzsche held that each centre of impulse, every so-called atom or monad, or what not, "strives to become master of all space, to extend its power, and to thrust back everything that resists it. But since it is constantly met by similar endeavours on the part of others, it comes to terms, that is combines, with those which are sufficiently related to it, in order to conspire for power together. And this process goes on and on."[1] Accordingly, Nietzsche sums up his view in the dictum : "This world is the Will to Power, and nothing else."[2]

The will to power may be seen most clearly, of course, in the conduct of men. "The love of power," says Nietzsche, "is the dæmon of mankind. You may give men everything possible—health, food, shelter, enjoyment—but they are, and remain, unhappy and capricious, for the dæmon waits and waits, and must be satisfied. Let everything else be taken away from men, but let this dæmon be satisfied, and then they will really be happy—as happy as men and dæmons can be."[3] And, in the same passage, Nietzsche makes another

---

[1] *The Will to Power,* vol. ii, § 636 (p. 121).
[2] *Ibid.,* § 1067 (p. 432); *Beyond Good and Evil,* § 36 (p. 52).
[3] *The Dawn of Day,* § 262 (p. 248).

hit at German Imperialism as a monstrous em-
bodiment of the will to power, and its readiness
to sacrifice everything else to it.   He parodies
some verses of Luther and perpetrates a pun on
the word *Reich*, which can mean either the King-
dom (of Heaven) or the (German) Empire :[1]

> " And though they take our life,
> Goods, honour, children, wife,
> Yet is their value small,
> These things shall vanish all,
> The *Kingdom* it remaineth."

Again, to return to Nietzsche's conception of
the centres of impulse, or of will to power.   The
use of such pluralistic expressions as "centres"
of impulse, or " points " of energy, etc., may
easily be misunderstood.   Nietzsche regards the
world as a *continuum*, as an unbroken flow of
energy, and not as composed of separate
"centres," " atoms," etc.   " There are no such
things," he writes, "as lasting and ultimate enti-
ties, no atoms, no monads . . . The notion of
' permanence ' was first introduced by ourselves
(from practical, utilitarian, and other motives)
. . . It is our constant striving for self-preserva-

[1] *The Dawn of Day,* § 262 (p. 248).

tion that necessitates our positing a rougher world of stable existences and things. We may speak of atoms and monads, but only in a relative sense.'' His favourite simile for the world is that of the sea. " It is energy everywhere, the play of forces and force-waves, at the same time one and many, rising here and falling there, a sea of forces, storming and raging, for ever changing . . . with an ebb and flow of its forms."[1]

Change, then, is of the essence of the cosmic process. And the changes are not fixed and stereotyped, but original and creative. The will to power is " a creative will."[2] " Becoming is inventing," it is " creative," it is " continual creativeness."[3] In one place Nietzsche speaks of the world as " a self-generating work of art."[4] The very fact that things are what is called "perishable" is, for Nietzsche, evidence of the world's " joy of unremitting creation " : things perish, that is to say, are broken up, in order that their elements may be put together again in ever new formations—as when a child pulls down its toy house in order to try new creations with the same

---

[1] *The Will to Power*, vol. ii, § 1067 (p. 431).
[2] *Thus Spake Zarathustra*, Part II—" Redemption " (p. 170).
[3] *The Will to Power*, vol. ii, §§ 617 (p. 108), 1059 (p. 424).
[4] *Ibid.*, § 796 (p. 239).

bricks.   Only, for Nietzsche, even the cosmic elements are not fixed, but changeable, spontaneously unstable.

The cosmic process, however, notwithstanding its creative instability, is not entirely lawless. Nietzsche does write sometimes as though he denied the existence of laws of nature.   In reality, however, he is only contesting laws conceived as though they were *imperatives* imposed upon things from outside, and formed no part of the intrinsic nature of the things themselves.   But modern science has never regarded the laws of nature as expressing anything else than the immanent nature of things.   And such laws Nietzsche admitted. He was rather foolishly taken in by the scientist's use of expressions like " Nature's conformity to law,"[1] which does not convey the scientist's meaning in the happiest fashion, but which most people understand all the same.

Again, the reality of Change involves the reality of Time, which Nietzsche considered to be infinite. Change, he asserts, is part of the essence of cosmic energy, therefore time is as well.[2]   As regards time, then, the world is infinite.   "This universe,"

---

[1] *Beyond Good and Evil*, § 22 (p. 32).
[2] *The Will to Power*, vol. ii, § 1064 (p. 427 f.).

he writes, " is a monster of energy, without beginning or end."[1]   Space, on the other hand, he regarded as finite, no part of it empty, but all filled with a fixed quantity of energy.[2]   The universe, in other words, is, according to Nietzsche, a finite quantity of energy, occupying a finite space, but infinite in its duration.

What may have induced Nietzsche to formulate the view of the finitude of space and of the amount of energy in the universe, it is not difficult to surmise.   It was most probably his acceptance and misinterpretation of the principle of conservation of energy.   Apparently he regarded the principle as futile if we assumed an infinity of energy : for in an infinite quantity of energy no loss or gain would be appreciable.   And if, now, the amount of energy in the universe is not to be thought of as infinite, it must also not be conceived as spread over an infinite space, for even a sparse distribution of energy through infinite space would still make the amount of energy infinite.   Consequently Nietzsche was led to regard both space and cosmic energy as limited in quantity.

This combination of ideas—the conception of

[1] *The Will to Power*, vol. ii, § 1067 (p. 431).
[2] *Ibid.*

the infinity of Time, and of the finitude of Space and Energy—brought Nietzsche round to the view of the world's Eternal Recurrence.   The doctrine may be stated briefly in Nietzsche's own words : " If the universe may be conceived as a definite quantity of energy, as a definite number of centres of energy . . . it follows that the universe must go through a calculable number of combinations in the great game of chance which constitutes its existence.   In infinity, at some moment or other, every possible combination must have been realized . . . And inasmuch as between every one of these combinations and its next recurrence every other possible combination would necessarily have been undergone, and since every one of these combinations would determine the whole series in the same order, a circular movement of absolutely identical series is thus demonstrated.   The universe is, therefore, shown to be a circular movement which has already repeated itself an infinite number of times, and which plays its game for all eternity.' "[1]

The world, again, is not particularly rational. " A *little* reason, to be sure, a germ of wisdom scattered from star to star—this leaven is mixed

[1] *The Will to Power*, vol. ii, § 1066 (p. 430).

in all things." But for the most part "wanton-
ness and folly" characterize the universe.[1] Even
the principle of contradiction may not be true of
the world of reality : it may only betray the im-
potence of man rather than reveal the nature of
the universe.[2]

Finally, the world, according to Nietzsche, has
no final purpose, and is guided by no "eternal
will " : it has no pre-determined purpose, and
tends towards no final state.[3] " If," he argues,
" the movement of the world tended to reach a
final state, then that state would already have been
reached '"—presumably because an infinity of
time has already elapsed, and therefore all possible
states of the universe have already been realized.

In this rather chaotic world, as Nietzsche con-
ceives it, our planet is, like every star, " without
plan and without reason." Life upon it is but
a passing incident, " something that is of no consequence to the general character of the earth."[4]
Even consciousness is of no special value to it.
" Consciousness, spirit, now seem to us rather a
symptom of relative imperfection in an organism,

---

[1] *Thus Spake Zarathustra*, Part III—"Before Sunrise" (p. 201).
[2] *The Will to Power*, vol. ii, § 515 (p. 30).
[3] *Thus Spake Zarathustra*, loc. cit.
[4] *The Will to Power*, vol. ii, § 708 (p. 177).
[5] Ibid., vol. i, § 303 (p. 248).

it is an experimenting, a groping . . . which absorbs an unnecessary quantity of nervous energy.'"[1] What is done unconsciously, instinctively, is done more perfectly than what is done consciously. In time consciousness may disappear entirely and " be superseded by perfect automatism.'"[2]

Nietzsche's outlook upon the world appears to be as cheerless and discouraging as is his theory of knowledge. He admits that there is something " extraordinarily gloomy and unpleasant " in his conception of the universe as " false, cruel, contradictory, seductive, and without sense.'"[3] He also realizes that " something in us rebels against this view," and " whispers to our hearts 'All this must be false because it is revolting.' " But he distrusts the still small voice. He suspects that it may only be the voice of "the serpent vanity.'"[4] Nietzsche's pessimistic bias, to which reference was made in the preceding chapter, seems to betray itself here also in his gloomy view of a chaotic and godless world. But—and this is one of the most striking features of his philosophy—his tragic conception of the universe does not turn him into

---

[1] *The Antichrist*, § 14 (p. 141).
[2] *The Will to Power*, vol. ii, § 523 (p. 38).
[3] *Ibid.*, § 853 (p. 289).
[4] *Ibid.*, vol. i, § 303 (p. 248).

a pessimist. On the contrary, it actually braces him, and heightens his conception of human life and destiny. The thought of what man has already achieved in spite of his unpromising lot amid inexorable forces, should inspire the race with an indomitable feeling of manly self-reliance, and stimulate them to unremitting efforts to mould the world nearer to the heart's desire.

The real significance of Nietzsche's theory of the universe is easily missed if special care is not taken to mark its connection with his philosophy of human life and conduct. To some extent one may say that Nietzsche's account of the universe gives us a picture of the world at its worst, while his ethical views show us how man might live an heroic life nevertheless. But that is not all. As will be explained fully in the next chapter, Nietzsche's ethical ideal is that of the full, heroic life; and such a life requires ample scope for its activities. Hence his inmost and fundamental objection to the conception of the world as completely mechanical, or as completely rational, or as under the full sway of a divine providence, or as otherwise pre-determined to reach some far-off and final goal. His rooted objection to any and all such views is that they tend to paralyse human effort, and so to impoverish human life, by fostering the belief that things are thus and thus, or will be thus and thus, quite independently of human strivings, which are therefore either unnecessary or futile. Looked at in this way it is not difficult to see why Nietzsche should have found something stimulating in his conception of an apparently chaotic and godless universe. Such a world, at all events, is a malleable world, a world still really in the making, where human effort really counts for something, and men are not mere puppets, whether tugged by merely mechanical wire-pullers, or surely and constantly guided by a divine stage-manager. Nietzsche had no patience with those who, for any of the foregoing reasons, were content to let their hands hang listlessly at their sides, leaving the world to itself, or to providence. It seemed to him unmanly to relax one's efforts on the plea (whether by way of despair, or by way of " faith ") that after all the world is what it is, and will be what it will be, with or without the meddling of mortal man. " The belief ' It is thus and thus,' " Nietzsche protested, " must be altered into the will ' Thus and thus shall it be.' "[1]   Man should brace himself, and wrestle with the hostile

[1] *The Will to Power*, vol. ii, § 593 (p. 98).

forces within and without, until he either masters them or perishes in the attempt. No numbing pessimism, and no indolent make-believe!

Nietzsche, moreover, had a special horror of the way in which the conception of God has often been used to the detriment of human life on earth. He was almost obsessed with the hostility of early Christianity against the world and the flesh. And it was this, more perhaps than anything else, that aroused his opposition to a religious conception of the universe. This point will be made clearer in the next chapter. But it may be remarked here that Nietzsche's philosophy is not so absolutely irreligious as may appear. After all, the conception of God which he opposed is not the only possible conception. Nietzsche himself has, in fact, suggested another conception of God in harmony with the rest of his philosophy. His conception combines the immanent, pantheistic view of God with the ideas of evolution and eternal recurrence. The resulting conception is that of a becoming God who is identical with the universe at each culminating stage of its development in the infinite course of its eternal recurrence. In other words, the universe in the course of its evolution becomes God whenever it arrives at the stage of maximum

F

power, and then ceases to be divine as it begins its course of declining or descending life, until it reaches again its zenith, and so on incessantly. " God " (says Nietzsche) " is the culminating moment : life is an eternal process of deifying and undeifying.'"[1]

Nietzsche's idea of God will, no doubt, be found perplexing by most people, though the conception of a " becoming God " is not altogether strange now.[2] But the point which I want especially to emphasize is that Nietzsche's philosophy is not really entirely anti-religious, quite apart from his admission of the legitimacy of current religious views for ordinary people. Nietzsche's theory of knowledge is rather favourable to such a conception of God as will tend to enrich life and to stimulate human effort. For if, as Nietzsche maintains, all that we can say about the best of our beliefs is that it helps life, then there is nothing to be said against, while much may be said for, such a conception of God as will help man to live the full life. In reality Nietzsche's objections apply, not to the belief in God absolutely, but only to that

---

[1] *The Will to Power,* vol. ii, § 712 (p. 181).
[2] The tendency to substitute the concept of " Final Cause " for that of " First Cause " (*see,* e.g., Ritchie's *Darwin and Hegel,* p. 75) implies the notion of a Becoming God.

conception of Him which represents Him as a kind of bogey, making man afraid of the world and of life; and also to that conception of God which discourages all strenuous effort by encouraging the belief that men can leave everything in His care, if only they pray, pray, pray. Such people, thinks Nietzsche, do not worship God, but something with long ears. Apart, however, from such views about God, which a great many religious people will readily admit to be erroneous, Nietzsche's philosophy is not necessarily ungodly. It already contains religious elements, which Nietzsche would probably have elaborated more fully had he been spared long enough to systematize his whole philosophy.

Before leaving the subject it may be advisable to refer briefly to a passage in Nietzsche's *Thus Spake Zarathustra*,[1] which has given rise to a good deal of misunderstanding. Zarathustra is made to say : " If there were Gods, how could I endure it not to be a God? Therefore there are no Gods." What could be more simple than to regard this as a bois- terous expression of Nietzsche's megalomania? The meaning, however, has nothing to do with Nietzsche's or anyone else's conceit. Nietzsche

[1] Part II—" In the Happy Isles," (p. 99).

had been considering for some time the hypothesis of a " becoming God " who is " unveiled more and more throughout the changes and fortunes of mankind.'" At the time of writing *Thus Spake Zarathustra,* when he was full of the idea of Eternal Recurrence and of the exhaustion of all possibilities in each of its cycles, he felt constrained to repudiate this conception of God because he thought that if the universe or mankind really could develop into a deity then the deification would have taken place before now, because an infinity of time must have elapsed already, and all possibilities must already have been realized. In the above utterance, I take it, Zarathustra simply voices this view in the name of humanity. If there could be a God, mankind would have attained to that position as part of the cosmic evolution. The view may be wrong, but it was not merely an expression of megalomania; and, as was explained before, Nietzsche subsequently dropped this view in favour of the conception of a becoming and periodically recurring, but non-permanent, or, at least, non-continuous Deity.

[1] *Human All-Too-Human,* vol. i, § 238 (p. 222).

CHAPTER VI

NIETZSCHE'S THEORY OF LIFE AND CONDUCT

WE now come to the most familiar part of Nietzsche's philosophy—his views on human life and conduct, and his conception of the superman. The fact that some of these views have become common property does not mean that they are properly understood. Rather it is due to their common misapprehension that Nietzsche's name has come into disrepute, and the conception of the superman has come to be regarded as the horrible vision of a supermaniac. To understand Nietzsche's real views one must dismiss all the usual prejudices. And then it may be found that his ethical theory contains much that is interesting and instructive, and very little, if anything, that is really offensive.

Nietzsche relates that he was barely thirteen years old when his boyish mind was already haunted by moral problems, notably the problem of evil. He was evidently not made to take things

for granted. And as he grew older he grew more
and more impatient with people who were content
to shuffle through life, without ever facing it with
open eyes, and deliberately saying to it either
" Yea " or " Nay."

His own views on life and conduct underwent
various changes. His conception of the world was
never exactly rose-coloured, and least of all so in
the earlier stages of his career. Accordingly we
find him at first a pessimist like Schopenhauer,
saying nay to life, and seeking refuge in art. It
is noteworthy that Nietzsche's artistic temperament and artistic way of looking at things never
entirely forsook him, but continued to the end to
colour his philosophic outlook, so that he conceived the whole cosmic process, and all the
activities of human life and knowledge as essentially akin to the creative work of the artist.
Nevertheless, art soon ceased to satisfy him as an
adequate solution to the riddle of existence. It
appeared to him, after a time, that art was no real
answer to the problems of life, but rather a way of
shirking its stern realities by playing with beguil-
ing phantasies. He felt that it was finer and more
manly to face the real world, and to unravel its
true character. Accordingly, we find him, for a

time, devoted to the pursuit of knowledge for its own sake, and esteeming even the smallest discoveries of the scientific spirit above the boldest flights of the artistic imagination. But this view likewise failed to satisfy him for very long. He felt chilled and repelled by the " wrinkled parchment faces " of the learned who looked upon life, but did not live. It occurred to him that merely to study life was not yet to live, and might only be another way of shirking or missing life itself. And so he arrived at his final view—the ideal of the fullest possible life. It was not enough, he thought, merely to see life truly, one should strive to live it whole.

Now the ideal of a fuller life was first impressed upon Nietzsche by his study of classic literature and of modern geniuses like Goethe. Nietzsche, like Carlyle, was a born hero-worshipper. And what impressed him most about the world's great heroes and geniuses was the greater fulness and intensity of their lives, as compared with the humdrum existence of ordinary mortals. As already remarked, it was his profound discontent with the pale cast of contemporary life and thought that prompted Nietzsche's philosophical enterprise. In the end he fairly succeeded in working out a theory of knowledge and of reality which constitute a suitable foundation for his views on life. But it is perhaps only just to remark that it was his views on life that influenced most the rest of his philosophy. Nietzsche would probably not have denied this. Only he might have pointed out, with considerable justice, that the same remark holds good of nearly all philosophies, for the key to most philosophies is to be found in their ethical portions. Moreover, he might have added that this was in complete accord with his own view that it is Life itself that seeks expression in all the activities of man, even in our most abstract and most remote philosophical speculations. Anyway, what comes last in the logical construction of a philosophic system, that is to say in its rational justification, may well come first in the actual mental life of the thinker as a mere suggestion or as an inspiration. Nietzsche cannot, therefore, be rightly accused of arguing in a circle, or of question-begging, because he bases his views on life upon his views on knowledge and reality, although, in another sense, it may be said that it was his views on life that gave a certain bias or direction to his other views.

As regards the general nature of man, Nietzsche holds that, like the rest of the universe, man consists of will to power, or centres of impulse or instinct struggling for mastery among themselves but still organized and united to a certain extent. What is commonly called the soul is simply the dominant centre, or subject, to which the rest are more or less subservient. " The assumption of a single subject," thinks Nietzsche, " is perhaps not necessary; it may be equally permissible to assume a plurality of subjects, whose interaction and struggle lie at the bottom of our thought and our consciousness in general. A sort of aristocracy of ' cells " in which the ruling power is vested.'"[2] Such a view might help to explain the phenomena of multiple personality, perhaps even death itself, according to Nietzsche.

Now, life-processes consist partly in a struggle of our whole organism, that is to say of our united instincts, with things outside us, and partly in a kind of civil strife among the instincts of the same organism. " Every instinct is a sort of thirst for power : each has its point of view, which it would fain impose upon all the other instincts as their norm.'"[3]

---

[1] This must not be regarded as evidence of Nietzsche's materialism. For Nietzsche there is no mere " matter," everything is " will to power."

[2] *The Will to Power*, vol. ii, § 490 (p. 18).

[3] *Ibid.*, § 481 (p. 13).

Again, consciousness (that is to say, explicit consciousness) occupies only a secondary place in the life of man. It is but the luminous surface of our stream of life, while the real work is carried on in the undercurrents of our sub-conscious instincts or blind impulses. The emergence of an instinct into consciousness, out of the nether currents of the stream of life, is comparable to the act of birth in the realm of biology. The act of birth is but a moment, an incident in the continuous process of hereditary transmission; and emergence into consciousness is but a moment, or an incident, in the instinctive life of men. This applies even to the most reflective thinking of a philosopher. " The greater part of the conscious thinking of a philosopher is secretly influenced by his instincts, and forced into definite channels. And behind all logic and its seeming sovereignty of movement there are valuations, or to speak more plainly, physiological demands, for the maintenance of a definite mode of life."[1]

This view of consciousness and conscious thinking shows the deeper reason, to which I alluded in the second chapter, why Nietzsche continued to write in aphorisms even when his health permitted

[1] *Beyond Good and Evil,* § 3 (p. 8).

of a fuller elaboration of his views. He did not put much faith in conscious reasoning, or dialectic. He believed that the instinctive forces which unconsciously and subconsciously prompted his conclusions might constitute a far stronger justification of them than anything that he could bring forward on their behalf on the surface of conscious thought. The conscious reason of man is referred to by Nietzsche as the "small reason," in comparison with the " great reason," or massive wisdom of the totality of human instincts through which Nature herself speaks to us, or prompts us.

Somewhat similar views have, of course, found favour with mystics and intuitionists and, to some extent, even with cold empiricists. Mill, for instance, tells, with approval, of the advice given to a man of sound common-sense, who had been appointed to a judicial post for which he had had no special training. The advice given to him was that he should give his decisions without stating his reasons, because his decisions (prompted by his instinctive common-sense) would probably be right, while his reasons would (in the absence of the necessary special training) as probably be wrong. Latterly, indeed, so much emphasis has been laid by numerous writers on the part played by the unconscious, or sub-conscious, that it would be quite gratuitous to defend Nietzsche's views on the subject against the charge of extravagance, even if one does not approve of this whole anti-rationalist tendency, or, at least, of the anti-intellectualist abuse of the " sub-conscious."

Some of Nietzsche's utterances have been rather foolishly misunderstood by those who did not know, or did not remember, his views on conscious thought and unconscious, or sub-conscious, instinct.   For example, in *Thus Spake Zarathustra*,[1] we read : " You ask me why?   I am not one of those who may be asked for their why !"   This is instanced by some critics as an expression of Nietzsche's conceit or megalomania.   But what he really meant is clear enough from the context.   The passage continues : " Is my experience but of yesterday?   It is long ago that I experienced the reasons for my opinions."   His opinions, in other words, were regarded by Nietzsche as the outcome of instinctive forces which had been working in him far back, though unconsciously ; and no reasons that he could consciously formulate would have done them justice.   The view may be wrong, but it is not an expression of mere conceit.

[1] Part II—" Poets " (p. 151 f.).

Nietzsche would say the same of everybody's opinions.

No doubt, from a strictly philosophical point of view, arguments based upon such unconscious or sub-conscious forces are rather suspect. They take one beyond the recognized province of philosophy into the realm of the obscure and the inarticulate, where it is not always easy to discriminate between the unutterably profound and the unspeakably nonsensical. Certainly one should be very sparing of such arguments. And Nietzsche himself has furnished an example which may well serve as a warning of the pestilence that walketh in the darkness of unreason. Nietzsche wrote that he felt " instinctively " certain that Shakespeare never wrote the works that bear his name, and that Bacon was their real author![1] Still, this must not blind us to the importance of the distinction between the foreground, or conscious part of the mind, and its background, or hinterland, where most of our instincts and energies operate effectively, if sub-consciously, and produce or stage-manage the play that is acted in the limelight of consciousness. Nietzsche, it is true, appears to underestimate the rôle of consciousness.

[1] *See* Georg Brandes' *Nietzsche* (p. 115).

But that is largely due to his exaggerated language. The fact that he propounds a philosophy at all, and even tries to persuade people consciously to adopt and pursue a certain ideal of life, shows that he did not really regard consciousness as a negligible byplay.

One regrettable result of Nietzsche's over-emphasis of the part played by unconscious forces in the deeper currents of life, is that he is sometimes betrayed thereby into the language of thorough-going determinism or fatalism. As against this tendency, however, the emphasis which he lays on the " creative " or spontaneous character of the " will to power " suggests rather the view of extreme in-determination or chance. And Nietzsche even speaks in the same breath of both chance and necessity as possibly characterizing the process of cosmic evolution in general, and the life of man in particular. " The iron hands of necessity," writes Nietzsche, " that shake the dice-box of chance continue their game indefinitely : hence it must happen that certain throws perfectly resemble every degree of appropriateness and good sense. It may be that our own voluntary acts and purposes are merely such throws, and that we are too circumscribed and

vain to conceive our extremely circumscribed
state! It may be that we ourselves shake the
dice-box with iron hands, and that even in our
most deliberate actions we do nothing but play
the game of necessity. Possibly! To rise beyond
this " possibly " we should have to be guests in
the underworld, playing at dice and betting with
Proserpine at the table of the goddess herself.'"
The way in which chance and necessity are
mated in this passage may appear strange. But
it is quite consistent with Nietzsche's views on the
nature of things. For, although each centre of
impulse has its own creative power, yet each is
limited in some way by the rest, some being by their
very nature more limited than others. Now these
very limitations introduce a large element of
necessity, while the creative spontaneity of each
introduces an element of chance. In any case,
Nietzsche finally and quite consistently, decided
in favour of a limited freedom of the will. "Sayest
thou," he remarks, " that nutrition, the land of
thy birth, air, and society, change thy will and
determine thee? Well, thy opinions do this to a
much greater degree, for they prescribe thy nour-
ishment, thy land of adoption, thy atmosphere,

¹ *The Dawn of Day,* § 130 (p. 137).

and thy society for thee.'"[1]   How thought can
effect all this, evidently perplexed Nietzsche.   It
seemed to him contrary to the principle of conservation of energy.   But he got over, or got round,
the difficulty by suggesting that thought "creates
new laws of motion in energy, though no new
energy," and that this might make it possible to
determine "new emotions and new desires in
men," without violating the principle of conservation of energy.[2]   Anyway, he fully realized that
only on the assumption of freedom (albeit a limited
freedom) could the problem of life and conduct
have any real significance.   For, on the supposition of thorough-going necessity, life and conduct,
and all that we think about them, would be pre-
determined; while, on the assumption of thorough-
going chance, nothing, and consequently not even
our best thought, could have any real bearing on
anything else.   The whole problem of life and
conduct is only of consequence on the supposition
that our thoughts about it are not entirely pre-
determined by irrational forces, but that we can
consider it on its own merits, and change ourselves,
to some extent at least, in accordance with the

[1] *Eternal Recurrence*, § 28 (vol. xvi, p. 251 f.).
[2] *Ibid.*, § 29 (p. 252).

fruits of our reflection.   Such was Nietzsche's
view.   He admitted human freedom, though he
insisted on its incompleteness.   " Learning," he
maintained, " alters us . . . But at the bottom
of our souls, quite ' down below,' there is certainly something unteachable, a granite of spiritual
fate, of pre-determined decision and answer to
pre-determined, chosen questions.'"   If further
information be asked for as to the extent to which
our knowledge, or our opinions, may alter us, or
may enable us to alter ourselves, Nietzsche's
answer is that " we can act as the gardeners of our
impulses."   We may cultivate and train our impulses or instincts in all sorts of styles.   Or we
may interfere with them only a little, " we may
let nature take its own course, only trimming and
embellishing a little here and there."   Or we may
deliberately abstain from meddling with them at
all, " we may allow them to spring up in accordance with their own natural growth and limitations, and fight out their battle among themselves,
nay, we may even take delight in such chaos—
though we may possibly have a hard time of
it !'"

---

[1] *Beyond Good and Evil,* § 231 (p. 181 f.).
[2] *The Dawn of Day,* § 560 (p. 388 f.).

G

Man, then, according to Nietzsche, is quite capable of a measure of self-culture—he can, to some extent, fashion himself and his destiny. So that the problem of life and conduct is, not a futile problem, but a real, live, significant problem— indeed, the most significant problem for man to face. Hence his insistent challenge : What say ye to life? Yea or Nay?

This challenge of Nietzsche's is not quite the same as the hackneyed question, " Is life worth living?" Nietzsche would have scorned this form of the problem. For it suggests that life can be evaluated, can be judged to have value or not, by some external, independent standard. And this Nietzsche denied. " The value of life," he in- sisted, " cannot be estimated " at all by reference to anything else.[1] For life itself is the ultimate standard and criterion of all our judgments. The only thing that we can really be sure of even in the case of the best of our beliefs is that they are useful to life. Life itself is the ultimate criterion of all our judgments. How, then, can we judge life by anything else? " Besides," adds Nietz- sche, " in order to approach the problem of the

[1] *The Twilight of the Idols*—" The Problem of Socrates," § 2 (p. 10).

value of life, a man would need to be placed outside life, and moreover know it as well as . . .
all who have lived it . . . When we speak of
values, we speak under the inspiration and through
the optics of life : life itself urges us to determine
values : life itself values through us when we determine values.''[1] Our attitude towards life is, therefore, something ultimate. We may cheerfully
embrace life, or spurn it, we may say Yea to it, or
Nay—but in either case we do so without any
external grounds, without the aid of external
reasons or valuations. If we say Yea to life, it
is not because we value it first and find it worth
while, but rather it is because we say Yea to it that
we find life worth living. Similarly, if we say
Nay to life, it is not because we find it worthless,
but rather it is because we say Nay to it that we
find it a burden. Indeed, even when we take up
an antagonistic attitude to life, it is still our life
itself that finds expression in our negative valuation
of it. Only in this case it is the expression of a
" declining, enfeebled, exhausted, and condemned
life . . . It is the instinct of degeneration itself
which converts itself into an imperative which says
' Perish !' It is the death-sentence of the man

[1] *The Twilight of the Idols*—" Morality," etc., § 5 (p. 30 f.).

who is already doomed."[1] For life is not only capable of growth, but is also subject to decline. And either process may be hastened and stimulated consciously and deliberately.

According to Nietzsche, then, life, or at all events ascending life, has unquestionable, ultimate value, and should be affirmed, as indeed it affirms itself, unconditionally. This, however, does not mean that all forms of life are of *equal* value. Far from it. All have some value, but their values vary enormously. What determines their degrees of value is the degree of fulness with which life is lived. The " superman " simply represents Nietzsche's ideal, or limiting conception, of the greatest possible fulness of human life.

Nietzsche's special pre-occupation with the superman, the hero, the genius, and those who have the making of such, or of approximations to them, has become a stumbling block to most people. Let it be said once for all that Nietzsche does *not* claim the world and the fulness thereof exclusively for supermen and their like. He does not propose to exterminate the mediocre, or to enslave them to the superior men, or even seriously to interfere with them in any way. On

[1] *The Twilight of the Idols*—" Morality," etc., § 5 (p. 30 f.).

the contrary, he insists that there is a natural order
of ranks among men, that the capacities and needs
of some men are by nature very different from
those of others. Whatever one's place may be in
this natural order of ranks it is not anything to be
either proud or ashamed of—it is just a fact to be
recognized. But it should be recognized, and not
ignored. For a man's whole outlook upon life and
reality must vary with his natural endowment,
and so will his conduct to some extent. The attempt to ignore these differences of nature has,
according to Nietzsche, only resulted in hypocrisy and in the impoverishment of life. People
for the most part do not live their natural lives,
but wear conventional masks, and play assumed
parts. Thanks to an unholy fear of Mrs. Grundy,

" All the world's a stage,
And all the men and women merely players."

And Nietzsche seems to have enjoyed the sport of
unmasking them.

If the natural order of ranks among men received due consideration, then it would be seen
that it is impossible to have the same code of conduct for all alike. And, again, if people only
realized that human conduct, and human valuations of conduct, are all subservient to life and its

needs, then they would see that, not only must different people have different codes of behaviour to suit their nature and circumstances, but also that the same people even require different codes of conduct at different times. Nietzsche devotes considerable space to show that this is what has actually happened in the history of mankind. " Everything good," he tries to show, " is the evil of yore which has been rendered serviceable."[1] And elsewhere he adds the following picturesque explanation. " Whoever " (he says) " has seen those furrowed basins which once contained glaciers, will hardly deem it possible that a time will come when the same spot will be a valley of woods and meadows and streams. It is the same in the history of mankind; the wildest forces break the way, destructively at first, but their activity was nevertheless necessary in order that later a milder civilization might build up its house. These terrible energies—that which is called evil—are the cyclopic architects and roadmakers of humanity."[2] Nietzsche's meaning is quite clear and unobjectionable. Nevertheless, his historical or pseudo-historical discussions of moral ideas have roused a good

---

[1] *The Will to Power.* vol. ii, § 1025 (p. 404).
[2] *Human All-Too-Human,* vol. i, § 24 (p. 228).

deal of righteous indignation. It is somehow
assumed that because Nietzsche tried to show that
cruelty and revenge, for instance, have rendered
good service in the early history of mankind, therefore he looked upon them as good even now. But
that is an absurdity of which he was certainly not
guilty. In fact, much too much has been made of
his historical or pseudo-historical digressions. These
excursions are not essential to his philosophy. For,
as he himself has insisted, and rightly insisted,
" an inquiry into the origin of our moral valuations
and tables of law has absolutely nothing to do with
the criticism of them, although people persist in
believing that it has.'" " A morality," he adds
elsewhere, "could even have grown out of an error :
but with this knowledge the problem of its worth
would not even be touched.'"

What, then, it may be asked, is the proper
standpoint from which to criticize or judge conduct? From what has already been said it should
be clear by now that, for Nietzsche, life itself constitutes the only right standpoint and basis of moral
judgment. But, it may be asked further, what
exactly does this imply?

---

[1] The Will to Power, vol. i, § 254 (p. 212).
[2] Joyful Wisdom, § 345 (p. 282).

In the first place, it implies that human life should not be made subordinate to anything else— not even to the hope of heaven, or to the fear of hell. Man's maxim, according to Nietzsche, should be, not *Memento mori*, but *Memento vivere!* His exhortation is : " Remain true to the earth, my brethren, with the power of your virtue! Let your bestowing love and your knowledge be devoted to be the meaning of the earth! . . . Let it not fly away from the earthly and beat against eternal walls! Ah! There hath always been so much flown-away virtue."[1] And again he urges : " Live so that thou mayest desire to live again," and not once again only, but an infinite number of times!'[2] Here we are shown the ethical motive of his doctrine of eternal recurrence. This doctrine helped to stress the importance of man's earthly existence, and to increase the gravity of the worldly problems of human life. Anyhow, the main point is clear. Just as Kant had insisted that man should be treated as an end, and not merely as a means, as a person and not merely as a tool, so Nietzsche urged that man's life on earth should be regarded as an end, not merely as a means, and

[1] *Thus Spake Zarathustra.* Part I, " The Bestowing Virtue," § 2 (p. 88).
[2] *Eternal Recurrence,* §§ 25, 27 (vol. xvi, p. 250 f.).

least of all as a purgatory. Many religious people will probably agree with Nietzsche to the extent of declining to consider the marring of the present life as the best way of meriting another.

In the second place, the appeal to life as the moral standard involves that whatever helps to make man's life fuller or richer must be judged good, and whatever tends to impoverish it must be considered bad. Now man, according to Nietzsche, is a bundle of instincts, or impulses, or centres of will to power, more or less organized. Consequently the more such instincts a man has, and the more completely they are organized, the fuller and better will his life be. As a limiting conception one may conceive someone endowed with the greatest number of instincts that it is possible for a man to have, and these of such strength as is compatible with their completely harmonious organization. Such a being would be Nietzsche's ideal superman.

One must be careful to note all the requirements or endowments of the superman—(1) wealth of instincts, (2) their strength, and (3) their harmonious organization. It is by ignoring the last of these conditions—to say nothing of Nietzsche's further demands that the superman should be clear-sighted and far-sighted—that Nietzsche's super-man has come to be caricatured by over-hasty critics as a kind of colossal bully. Goethe was probably the nearest approach to Nietzsche's ideal. Napoleon much less so, for Nietzsche referred to him as a combination of the "*super*human" with the "*in*human." What has helped to prejudice good folk against the superman is the fact that Nietzsche frequently describes him in terms of "power." The word naturally suggests at once brute strength. But, for Nietzsche, every instinct or capacity is a power, a "will to power." And if he had only described his superman as one endowed with a wealth of great capacities completely co-ordinated, he might have met with less prejudice and more understanding.

By the superman, then, Nietzsche meant the fullest possible realization of a complete, self-reliant personality. "The majority of people" (thinks Nietzsche) "are only piecemeal and frag-mentary specimens of man."[1] Their capacities and their interests are very restricted and stunted. They are not "all-round" men. Speaking meta-phoricallly, Nietzsche says : "One person lacks an eye, another an ear, a third a leg ; yet others a

[1] *The Will to Power,* vol. ii, § 881 (p. 317).

tongue, nose, or—head!" Nay, he has seen even worse things than such cripples, namely, "reversed cripples," that is to say, people who only have one thing, and too much of that—" men who are nothing more than a big eye, or a big mouth, or a big belly, or something else big." He has seen " an ear as big as a man . . . perched on a small, thin stalk—the stalk, however, was a man! People said that the big ear was not only a man, but a great man, a genius. . . . But it was only a reversed cripple who had too much of one thing and too little of everything else. . . . I find man broken up, and scattered about as on a battlefield, or in shambles . . . fragments and limbs and fearful mishaps—but no men!" No complete men.[1]

What is the reason of this dearth of whole men? Nietzsche thinks that it is because little or nothing has been done to make such complete men possible, while much has been done to make them impossible. And in this respect Christianity has sinned most, according to Nietzsche. Its contempt for the world and the flesh, and its idealization of all that makes man anæmic and sickly, stand in the way of more robust ideals, such as the Greeks pursued.[2] " Virtue," as

---

[1] *Thus Spake Zarathustra*, Part II, " Redemption " (p. 166 f.).
[2] *The Antichrist*, § 22 (p. 151); *The Will to Power*, vol. i, § 361 (p. 291), etc.

commonly conceived, he complains, " is turning
the world into a hospital, so that everybody may be
everybody else's nurse."[1] Of course, Nietzsche
had his own views of the extent to which Christen-
dom is really Christian, and the extent to which it
is still pagan. But the form of the compromise
which he saw around him did not please him.
" The life of modern man " (he says contemptuously) " is passed in see-sawing between Christianity and Paganism, between a furtive or hypo-
critical approach to Christian morality, and an
equally shy and spiritless dallying with the antique ;
and he does not thrive under it."[2] There is a pain-
ful absence of sincerity in modern culture as compared with Greek culture. In fact, modern culture
is only " a decoration of life—a concealment and
disfigurement of it." And Nietzsche pleads for
greater sincerity in life and conduct as a step towards genuine culture, even if such sincerity should
" shatter a whole system of merely decorative
culture."[3]

The ideal state of man, as Nietzsche conceived
it, is that of the superman. The superman is per-

---

[1] *The Will to Power*, vol. i, § 395 (p. 316).

[2] *Thoughts of Season*, vol. ii—" Schopenhauer," § II (p. 112 f.)

[3] *Ibid.*, " The Use and Abuse of History," *ad fin.* (p. 199 f.).

fectly sincere : he is what he appears to be, and
appears as he is. He is perfectly natural; his life
is autonomous and spontaneous. He does the right
thing spontaneously, not because of any commands
dictated to him by others; and he abstains from
what is wrong simply because he is wholly occupied
with doing what is right, and not in obedience to
any externally imposed " Don't." With the
ordinary man it is different. He is largely, if not
wholly, dependent on the opinion and example of
others. He respects, or professes to respect, externally prescribed norms, and is especially haunted
by externally imposed prohibitions.

There is a story which Nietzsche would probably
have used to illustrate this aspect of his ethical
doctrine, if he had only known it. A little girl, it
is related, was asked her name. She replied,
" Mary." Again she was asked, " Mary what?"
The girl paused for a moment, and then said :
" Mother always calls me ' Mary Don't.' " This
story would probably have been regarded by
Nietzsche as a concise expression of the average
Hebrew's and Christian's conception of his rela-
tion to his Father in Heaven ever since Adam and
Eve Don't were expelled from the Garden of
Eden. Such a negative mode of life is not at all to

Nietzsche's taste.   It is poles asunder from his ideal of conduct.

At the same time, it cannot be said too emphatically that Nietzsche explicitly recognized the need of externally imposed codes of conduct for ordinary mortals, although he maintained that it is far wiser to dwell on what should be done than on what should be left undone.   " In the main (he wrote) all those moral systems are distasteful to me which say : ' Do not do this !   Renounce !   Overcome thyself !'   On the other hand, I am in favour of those moral systems which stimulate me to do something, to do it again from morn till eve, and dream of it at night, and think of nothing else but how to do it *well*, as well as it is possible for me alone !   From him who so lives there fall away one after another the things that do not pertain to his life.   Without hatred or antipathy he sees this leave him to-day, and that to-morrow. . . . Or he does not see at all that they leave him—so firmly is his eye fixed on his goal, forward, not sideways, or backward, or downward.   What we do must determine what we leave undone ; in that we do some things we leave others undone. . . . But I do not mean to strive deliberately for my impoverishment : I do not like any of the negative virtues

whose essence is negation and self-renunciation.'"[1]
He believed in " Olympus, not in man on the
Cross.'"[2]

Even the superman, however, cannot retain all
his instincts, or develop equally such as he does
retain. Some of his instincts must, so to say,
shrivel up from sheer disuse, while others can only
be allowed a subordinate place in the organization
of his life, in which only a certain number of instincts can be predominant and fully cultivated. It
should be carefully noted that the superman, as
conceived by Nietzsche, does not let his impulses
grow wild. He is their gardener, cultivating
some, pruning and training others, and utterly
neglecting the rest. He cultivates his garden, and
is complete master of himself. And the " cultivation " of the instincts, it is especially worth noting,
includes also their " spiritualization." Sensuality,
for example, is spiritualized into love. Hostility
(to take another example) is spiritualized when we
no longer desire the annihilation of our enemies,
but realize the value of having rivals, so that, in
political life, for instance, we are occasionally con-
fronted by the spectacle of the opposition coming

[1] *Joyful Wisdom,* § 304 (p. 238 f.).
[2] *The Will to Power,* vol. ii, § 1034 (p. 407).

to the rescue of the party in power, or the party in power saving the opposition from going to pieces.   And so forth.[1]

Again, what characterizes the superman is, not ruthless self-indulgence, as some suppose, but severe self-discipline.   The natural spontaneity of his behaviour is not the outcome of a go-as-you-please policy, but the fruit of long training. "Every artist" (says Nietzsche) "knows how different from the state of letting oneself go is his 'most natural' condition, the free arranging, locating, disposing, and constructing, in the moments of ' inspiration '—and how strictly and delicately he then obeys a thousand laws which . . . defy all formulation by means of concepts.'"[2] So it is with the art of living.

Nor is the superman's external behaviour necessarily different from that prescribed by the usually accepted norms of good conduct.   Nietzsche states explicitly, " I should not, of course, deny—unless I were a fool—that many actions which are called immoral should be avoided and resisted; and, in the same way, that many which are called moral should be preferred and encouraged; but I hold that in

---

[1] *The Twilight of the Idols*—" Morality," etc., § 3 (p. 28 f.).
[2] *Beyond Good and Evil*, § 188 (p. 107).

both cases these actions should be performed from other motives than those which have prevailed to the present time.'"[1] For example, the superman is *not* ruthlessly selfish, but shows consideration for others, and is more lenient with those who are weak than with himself or his like. But he helps the weak and the unfortunate, not from sheer sentimental pity or a sickly sensitiveness to pain, but rather because his superabundance of power generates in him an impulse to help where he can help, to improve whatever needs improvement.[2]

Nietzsche's denunciation of the cult of suffering is easily mistaken for brutality. But that is a stupid mistake. It should be remembered that Nietzsche suffered much throughout his life. His opposition to an excessively tender attitude towards suffering was, therefore, not merely an expression of that insensitiveness to other people's pain which one sometimes meets with among those who have never suffered themselves. No, it just showed his indomitable spirit of independence and courage. In his eyes " manliness " was the highest virtue— " virtue " in its original sense. He wishes to see cultivated what he called " a sense for the tragic,"

---

[1] *The Dawn of Day*, § 103.
[2] *Beyond Good and Evil*, §§ 260 (p. 228), 293 (p. 259).

that is, the ability to face life like a hero, to bear
" the thousand ills that flesh is heir to " without
complaining, and not to spare oneself in the fight
for some great, impersonal cause.[1] " My suffering (exclaims Zarathustra) and my fellow-suffer-
ing, what do they matter! Do I, then, strive
after *happiness?* I strive after my *work.*"[2]

Nietzsche has written much and enthusiastically
about the superman (alias genius, hero, etc.), and
his name has come to be almost wholly identified
with the conception of the superman. Hence,
quite apart from the current misconceptions as to
what Nietzsche really meant by it, there is a general
impression that the character of the superman was
intended to be an immediate ideal for everybody.
It is easy enough to see the seductiveness of the
twofold misinterpretation for some people. Many
a bully, militarist and otherwise, must have found
it very flattering to think of himself as a kind of
superman, the incarnation of a new philosophical
ideal. But that is a brutal mistake, the likely
occurrence of which Nietzsche foresaw, and tried to
forestall. "Independence" (he protests), "free development, and *laisser aller* are clamoured for most

---

[1] *Thoughts out of Season,* vol. i—" Richard Wagner in Bayreuth," § IV (p. 130 f.).
[2] *Thus Spake Zarathustra.* End of Part IV (p. 402).

vehemently precisely by those for whom no restraint could be too severe.''[1] Anyhow, Nietzsche had not the remotest intention to try to impose indiscriminately one universal ideal in place of another. He did not believe in *universal* ideals suitable for all alike. '' Whatever ideal one may have '' (he said) '' one should not insist on its being *the* ideal.''[2] One of the principal points of his whole polemic was that there is a natural order of ranks among men, and that one and the same ideal or standard of conduct must not be imposed upon all alike. His polemic against Christian or current moral ideas was not really directed against them as such, but only against their *tyranny*, against their claim to be the sole moral ideals, and their indiscriminate application to all sorts of people irrespective of their natural order of rank. Nietzsche knew of but extremely few approximations to the superman in history, and he could not flatter any of his contemporaries as such approximations. It would, therefore, require some temerity to consider oneself fit for that ideal. At one time, indeed, Nietzsche thought that the superman might only be evolved out of man by a long and slow process

---

[1] *The Twilight of the Idols*—'' Skirmishes,'' etc., § 41 (p. 100).
[2] *The Will to Power*, vol. i, § 349 (p. 100).

of evolution similar to that by which man has evolved out of the ape. But he modified his view, and finally thought of the superman as an ideal to which men of the higher natural ranks could approximate more and more, and in ever increasing numbers, if only the rest of humanity did not try to tyrannize over them, and keep them down to their own level, by compelling them to submit to common ideas and ideals.

Nietzsche's antipathy against Christianity and Democracy was partly due to their insistence on the equality of men. He himself believed that men are not, and never will be, equal. The doctrine of the equality of mankind, and the morality based upon it, were regarded by Nietzsche as responsible, in large measure, for the shortage of great personalities. Hitherto, he held, it has taken a whole nation to produce six or seven great men.[1] If people would only learn to appreciate the intrinsic worth of great men, then they would consciously and deliberately strive to make conditions more favourable for the rise of great individualities (or supermen) in ever growing numbers. And this very work of preparation would imbue all ranks with a new interest in life, and a new dignity. To

[1] *Beyond Good and Evil*, § 126 (p. 94).

persuade men to take up this task, was Nietzsche's self-imposed mission. But he did not mean to impose the same ideal on all alike. On the contrary, he wanted each man to realize his true place in the natural order of ranks, and to make the best of it honestly, cheerfully, and without vain conceits or regrets. " A capable artisan or scholar " (Nietzsche held) "cuts a good figure if he have pride in his art, and looks pleasantly and contentedly upon life. On the other hand, there is no sight more wretched than that of a cobbler or a schoolmaster who, with the air of a martyr, gives one to understand that he was really born for something better. There is nothing better than . . . to have a certain kind of capacity, and to use it. This is *virtù* in the Italian style of the Renaissance."[1]

As regards the natural order of ranks among men, Nietzsche distinguished broadly two principal ranks, which he designated respectively as (1) "masters," and (2) "slaves"—a rather unfortunate designation. By (1) " masters," he meant those exceptional people who are by nature virile and self-reliant; while by (2) " slaves," he meant mediocre people, who are by nature rather weak,

[1] *The Will to Power*, vol. i, § 75 (p. 64 f.).

and dependent upon others in matters of opinion, conduct, etc.   To which of these main types one happens to belong is not really a matter either for praise or for blame, but just a fact to be honestly faced.   The exceptional man has a right to live his own life, and the mediocre his.

It is to the exceptional men, the "master" souls, to whom Nietzsche looks chiefly for the realization of his ideal superman.   They must strive towards that ideal by submitting to rigorous self-discipline.   But the mediocre, too, may live useful and happy lives in their own way.   "For the mediocre" (Nietzsche thought) "it is a joy to be mediocre. . . . It would be absolutely unworthy of a profound thinker to see any objection in mediocrity *per se*.   For in itself it is the first condition under which exceptions are possible, and a high culture is determined by it."   It was obviously not Nietzsche's intention that the superman should tyrannize over the mediocre or even exploit them in any way.   The mediocre were to live contented and happy lives, and nothing was to be done, whether by supermen or others, to make their lot wretched.   Hence Nietzsche was furious with the "socialistic rabble" because they "undermine the working-man's instinct, his happiness and contentedness with his insignificant existence, they make him envious and teach him revenge.'"[1]

Nietzsche respected the unpretentious mediocre, and would not have them thwarted, or interfered with, in any way. Let them, by all means, retain their "herd-morality," their ideal of "green-pasture happiness," and even their religious views. "There are sober and industrious people," Nietzsche remarked, "on whom religion is embroidered like a hem of higher humanity; these do well to remain religious, it beautifies them.'"[2] And as to emancipating oneself from the yoke of current moral ideals, Nietzsche warns us that the really important consideration is, not what one is free *from*, but what one is free *for*—what new ideals one is putting in the place of the old. "Free dost thou call thyself? " Zarathustra asks. "Thy ruling thought would I hear about, and not that thou hast escaped from a yoke. Art thou entitled to escape from a yoke? Many a one hath cast away his final worth when he cast away his servitude.'"[3]

Nietzsche, then, did not mean his ideal of the superman for universal adoption. Much nonsense

---

[1] *The Antichrist,* § 57 (p. 219 f.).
[2] *Human All-Too-Human,* vol. i, § 115 (p. 124).
[3] *Thus Spake Zarathustra,* Part I—"The Way of the Creating One " (p. 71).

has been said and written about Nietzsche's "immoralism." But it is all due to a misapprehension both of what he really meant by "superman," and for whom the ideal was intended.

At the same time, it may be remarked, the conception of an ideal intended for the elect few is not free from difficulties. It may be urged with some justice that an ultimate ideal of human life, if it has any validity at all, should be valid for all in some measure. Nietzsche would probably not have denied this entirely. There are passages in his writings which rather support the contention. But, in that case, what becomes of his insistence on the different natural orders of rank and their several moralities? The answer is, that Nietzsche regarded the moralities of the lower ranks as stages of development on the way to the higher ideals of the superman. So long as people really belong to the lower ranks of the species, they are not fit for the higher ideal, which would only be misunderstood to their own undoing. Such people have greater worth by conforming to custom and convention. But, on the other hand, Nietzsche, notwithstanding his sanguine faith in heredity, did not believe in the fixity of the ranks of men. A man's rank is chiefly determined by what he himself is, not

by what his father and forefathers were. "Hence-
forth," exclaims Nietzsche, "let it be your
honour, not whence ye come, but whither ye go!
. . . Not backward shall your nobility gaze, but
onward."[1] If so, then one never can tell from a
man's birth into a certain station of life whether
his is a master-nature, or no. In the last resort,
one is led to suppose, the individual must decide
for himself, and take the consequences. After all,
the ideal of the superman, conceived as Nietzsche
conceived it, is not a soft option, but a severe dis-
cipline.

Moreover, there is something in Nietzsche's
ideal which may well appeal to a great many people
who have no vain delusions about their capacity to
realize it. The conception of a full, courageous,
and spontaneous individuality has a message for
everybody of intelligence and spirit. Hence we
need not be surprised to find that, in spite of
Nietzsche's professed aristocratic leanings and his
open contempt for socialism and democracy, the
gospel of superman has touched a sympathetic
chord even among democrats. Nietzsche probably
misunderstood the inmost meaning of democracy

[1] *Thus Spake Zarathustra*, Part III—" Old and New Tables,"
§ 12 (p. 248).

and socialism. Notwithstanding a certain amount of clap-trap about the equality of men, which Nietzsche loathed so much and rightly denied, what democracy is really aiming at, and helping to bring about, is greater opportunities for a more extensive cultivation of individuality. Its inmost and growing purpose is, not that all men should be alike, but that all alike should have an opportunity of cultivating each his own individuality, according to the measure of his endowment. And that purpose is after Nietzsche's own heart. It has also been shown already, in the first chapter, that Nietzsche warmly appreciated the tendency of democracy to put an end to international animosities, so that mankind may devote its whole energy to higher things than brutal warfare, and nations and peoples may stimulate and help, instead of obstructing and slaughtering, one another. So that, after all, the spirit of modern democracy and the spirit of Nietzsche's philosophy are not so opposed as is often asserted. Nor, as I have tried to show in the first chapter, do his views on the future of mankind and their international relations contain anything but what may be regarded as a consummation devoutly to be wished.

INDEX